A PRIEST FOREVER

The Life and Times of Father Robert McNamara

Ann K. Maloney

ISBN: 978-1-4834-1876-6 (sc)
ISBN: 978-1-4834-1875-9 (e)

Library of Congress Control Number: 2014917110

Because of the dynamic nature of the Internet, any web addresses or links contained in
this book may have changed since publication and may no longer be valid. The views
expressed in this work are solely those of the author and do not necessarily reflect the
views of the publisher, and the publisher hereby disclaims any responsibility for them.

Any people depicted in stock imagery provided by Thinkstock are models,
and such images are being used for illustrative purposes only.
Certain stock imagery © Thinkstock.

Lulu Publishing Services rev. date: 10/17/2014

In memory of
Helen Dwyer McNamara
(1867-1956)
who told Father Bob
"You have been a good son."

Foreword

It is with great pleasure that I am writing this foreword for *A Priest Forever: The Life and Times of Father Robert McNamara*. I first met Father Bob when I was a student at St. Bernard's Seminary in 1957. During the two years I was there, I had him as a teacher. I always found him to be committed to his subject and students. He was also very gracious, humble, and kind.

When I was in Rome at the North American College I read his book about that institution. I thoroughly enjoyed reading it and it helped me understand the workings of the college.

I became reacquainted with him in 1979 when I came to Rochester to shepherd the Roman Catholic Diocese of Rochester. Upon arriving one of the first things I did was to read Father Bob's book on the Diocese of Rochester. This book, like the one on the North American College, gave me a good insight into the workings of the diocese. Both of these books are considered outstanding pieces of American Catholic institutional history.

After I became Bishop, I enjoyed a positive on-going relationship with Father Bob. I was always amazed at the number of people who contacted him and requested his assistance in historical matters and matters of church buildings and decorations. He was always remarkably generous in his response to such requests.

I can tell you that our diocese owes Father McNamara a great debt of gratitude for preserving our history. It was he who had the idea of establishing the diocesan archives. He not only had the idea, he rolled up his sleeves and worked on it, so that the archives are a reality today. Future generations will benefit from his idea.

On a personal note, I can state Father Bob is an extraordinary man. Our diocese is much the richer for his priesthood and person.

+Matthew H. Clark
Bishop of Rochester
August 5, 2003

Preface

As I grew up in Corning, New York, I always knew my mother had a cousin in Rochester, New York, who was a priest and whose name was Father Robert Francis McNamara. I also knew he taught at St. Bernard's Seminary in Rochester and had written a book titled *A Century of Grace* about his home parish, St. Mary's in Corning. Father Bob had given an autographed copy of this book to my parents. I always thought that it was pretty cool to have such a distinguished relative.

I never really knew Father Bob, however, until October 1987, when I moved to Rochester for my job with the New York State Office of Children and Family Services. I phoned my cousin after I settled in, and asked if I could come out to say hello. He said, "Sure." We went out to Crescent Beach Restaurant for dinner. That was the beginning of a long and beautiful friendship.

I also knew I had a relative in Corning named Dr. Thomas L. McNamara. He was Father Bob's half-brother and had two daughters, Kathy and Sue. Although there was a considerable age difference among us (39.5 years between Father Bob and me, and four years between Sue and me), we proved to be kindred spirits. Little did Sue and I expect at that time that we would undertake a venture which would bear fruit for years to come. This venture would be to write, illustrate, and publish a little biography of Father Bob. Although we began while he was alive, Father went home to the Lord on May 22, 2009.

Both Sue and I came to believe there was a reason, beyond our understanding, why we were producing this book. Our belief stemmed from the fact that it had taken me well over a year to obtain Father Bob's permission. The first few times I asked him, his response was a flat-out "no." When I persisted, he argued that almost everyone who had known him well was dead, so that there were few who could be interviewed; that I had never written a book, no easy task; and that Sue, although an excellent photographer, had little experience in graphic design. Finally, however, on December 4, 2002 – which would have been my late mother's 94th birthday – our family priest broke down. "All right," he said, "but you are on your own." I've often wondered if Mom herself had something to do with changing his mind. Perhaps she did, for she held him in high regard.

When I called Sue to tell her, she was thrilled. We decided the best way for us to work together was for me to do the writing and Sue the pictures and overall design. As we talked, we even dared to think our proposal had been a divine inspiration! We figured that when people read a book by two amateurs like Sue McNamara TenEyck and Ann Maloney, some of them, at least, might join us in stumping for priestly and religious vocations.

We hoped, too, that our book could encourage others who might be discerning a religious vocation to accept it without fear. In an article published in Rochester's *Catholic Courier* of May 24, 2001, Father Bob called his priesthood "a radiant privilege." "My constant prayer is that every young man who hears [God] calling will answer 'yes'." Both Sue and I have joined him in his daily prayer and we invite you, the reader, to do the same. Today the number of Catholic priests and nuns is disturbingly low.

One of my friends has commented that the book, written at a time when the Roman Catholic Church has been experiencing a clerical crisis, would remind readers that the overwhelming majority of priests serve with decency and dedication. In presenting Father Robert's story, we intend to set forth the example of one contemporary priest who is a model of compassion and commitment to his calling -- a shining light to others. The main task of such biographies, therefore, is to locate "a cloud of witnesses" (Heb. 12:1).

Bishop Clark has called Father McNamara "an extraordinary man." Having rediscovered the man himself, and the opinion of those who have known him well, we believe that *A Priest Forever* will justify the Bishop's assessment.

Ann K. Maloney
Susan M. McNamara-Ten Eyck
August 2012

Acknowledgements

Many people were involved in the making of this book. These included priests, seminarians, religious, lay people, and sometimes whole families. For want of space we list by name only the major contributors.

- Rev. Robert C. Bradler; Rev. Joseph P. Brennan; Bishop Matthew H. Clark; Rev. Francis R. Davis; Cardinal Timothy Dolan; Rev. William E. Graf; Rev. Joseph A. Hart; Rev. Thomas D. Hoctor; Msgr. Gerard C. Krieg; Rev. Robert C. MacNamara; Msgr. J. Emmett Murphy; Rev. Celestine Obi; Rev. Jasper G. Pennington; Rev. John J. Philipps; Rev. John T. Reif; Msgr. William H. Shannon; Rev. Conrad J. Sundholm. "Father Mac" himself, of course, read the manuscript in progress, checking for correctness and completeness.
- Sr. Connie Derby, R.S.M.; Sr. Kathleen Milliken, R.S.M.; Sr. Roberta Rodenhouse, R.S.M.; Sr. Anna Louise Staub, S.S.J.; Sr. Mary Sullivan, R.S.M.
- Mrs. Jeanne Marie Bello; Mrs. Ellen Brannin; Judge and Mrs. Arnold Ciaccio; Mr. and Mrs. William Doran; Mrs. Lois Janes; Dr. Joseph G. Kelly; Mr. E. Leo McMannus; Ms. Mary Napoleon; Ms. Victoria Schmitt; Mrs. Virginia Stevens; Mrs. Ida Turan and Mr. Samuel F. Turan; Ms. Kathleen Urbanic; Mr. E. Robert Vogt.

Sue and I thank each one of you, named or unnamed, for your assistance. Without your help this book would have remained a dream. May God bless you all.

Special Acknowledgements

In every endeavor that is worth undertaking there will always be extra acknowledgements that need to be mentioned. Father Bob's book is no exception. I certainly can take credit for the research and writing but I also want to acknowledge publicly a few others who made important contributions to the project. These are:

First: The Holy Trinity who gave me the courage, persistence, and ability to work on this endeavor. While I always hoped that Father Bob would live long enough to see the conclusion of our project, I thank God that my cousin lived long enough to work on the part of the book that only he could do; this was the part regarding his early life.

And the rest, in alphabetical order:

Reverend Robert Bradler: Father Bradler was the pastor at St. Thomas the Apostle Church when Father Bob lived at the rectory there. When my cousin first gave me his permission to write this book, Father Bradler held a meeting at St. Thomas and invited people to come and share their recollections and stories of Father McNamara with me. It was at this meeting that we came up with the title for the book.

Ellen Brannin: Ellen came to know Father Bob when he lived at St. Thomas the Apostle. She aided him in his writings for *Saints Alive* and in the writing of his last book, *Good Old Doctor Mac*. Ellen was a wonderful support to me at the time of Father's Bob's death and subsequent cleaning out of his rooms. In addition, Ellen provided me with much needed technical computer support.

Reverend William Graf: Father Bill was my cousin's very good friend. When I started doing interviews he gave me some valuable information which I later incorporated into the book. During Father Bob's last illness, he provided much spiritual and emotional support to both my cousin and me. In addition, he was always available for any questions that arose in the course of writing the book.

Susan M. McNamara TenEyck: Sue, who is Father Bob's niece, is responsible for the photo layout of the book. She collected all the pictures, obtained the necessary permissions for usage, and created a pictorial life of Father Bob which complements the text. In addition, Sue played another part. Every time I became discouraged or frustrated she allowed me to cry and whine on her shoulder, and then provided encouragement to complete the book.

Kathleen Urbanic: Kathy is an author herself and in that role she understood, in ways I did not, what editing means. Kathy gave a great deal of time editing the manuscript, at no expense to me, so it would be clear and concise.

Sister Mary Frances Wegman, R.S.M.: Sister Fran is the head of the Independent Living Center for Seniors (ILS) at the Mercy Center (formerly the Motherhouse). She was the person who brought Father Bob into the Mercy Center and, along with her staff, provided him with excellent care. I believe it was this care that gave my cousin the time, strength, and energy to write the book about his father and help me begin this biography.

I thank each and every one of you for your assistance in this endeavor. I know Father Bob thanks you, too.

Credits

- Photo of interior, Church of Santa Maria dell' Umiltà, Rome, Italy: permission to use given by Fotografia Felici.
- Georgetown University Archives provided a copy of the speech Father Bob gave on the occasion of his twenty-fifth anniversary of ordination.
- North American College Archives provided a copy of a 1956 photo of the chapel.
- Patrick Crowe: cover photo of Father Bob.
- Photo of Father Bob with Jeanne Marie Bello and Mary Meagher Tehan: permission given by Ms. Bello and Ms. Tehan.

Contents

CHAPTER ONE

Presenting Father Bob

There is something reassuring about light. It helps us find our way through the darkness. We continue our journey bravely when we see "light at the end of a tunnel." Light also multiplies itself as the moon mirrors the sun.

Scripture naturally praises light, the enemy of darkness. Jesus tells us, "I am the light of the world" (John 8:12).[1] In the gospel of Luke, we also read the parable in which he states, "No one who lights a lamp hides it away or places it under a bushel basket, but on a lamp stand so that those who enter might see the light" (Luke 11:33). Jesus thus indicates that those who receive his light are expected to shine it for all to see.

I have often speculated about what has so attracted me to my priestly cousin, Father Robert F. McNamara, and why I was so intent to write a book about him. I have often wondered whether other people saw in him the uniqueness that I did. I began to formulate my answer after reading a thoughtful passage by Elizabeth-Anne Stewart: [2]

> "Occasionally, we encounter those rare individuals whose very presence radiates light. This light has nothing to do with physical appearance, intellectual abilities, or manner of dress; it is a manifestation of the person's unique relationship with his or her divine source. In fact, one could say that this light is nothing less than God's presence shining through a human vessel, not

---

[1]   All Biblical references are taken from New American Bible.
[2]   "Living Faith," *Creative Communications for the Parish,* Jan. 2, 2005.

to glorify the person but to invite others to examine their own spiritual commitment."

After I read this entry, I began to understand that what I saw in Father Bob was his commitment to God; I saw how God used him as a very human vessel through which to shine or reflect divine light. I began to examine my own relationship with God, and I have become more aware of my duty to set a good example for others in my own Christian life. When I started to interview people for this book, I soon realized that many others saw this esteemed Catholic priest and teacher as one who was a lens and reflector of Christ.

How did I initiate my search for information about my subject?

First, I sent out a form letter to many people who knew Father Mac. (They all responded: surely a good sign.) Several were fellow priests, including Matthew H. Clark, the bishop of Rochester, who graciously agreed to write the book's foreword. I also contacted a number of lay people who benefited from Father Bob's professional aid, including Mrs. Sandy Doran and Ms. Kathleen Urbanic. Both of them are archivists, and so is Sr. Connie Derby, director of archives for the Rochester Diocese. (Biographers *have* to turn to archivists for details!)

These interviews, of course, taught me much about Father that I had not known. I learned that he wrote not only historical narratives, religious and secular, but also appealing meditations on the Rosary. I learned, too, of some of his private characteristics: how he became a father figure to one young relative, subsidizing her education when her own father was unable to do so. Many of his friends have likewise testified to his constant practice of giving credit for the good deeds of people who were better known for their follies.

Next, I contacted the archives at Georgetown University in Washington D.C., the Pontifical North American College in Rome, the Corning-Painted Post Historical Society, the Steuben County Historical Society, and the archives of the Rochester Diocese. All of these institutions with which he was connected sent me data that indicated the breadth of his activities. Georgetown, for example, mailed me a copy of the commencement sermon he gave there in 1952. The North American College submitted material he had collected while writing the history of that Roman center. The

Rochester diocesan archives bear witness not only to his teaching career but also to the assistance he gave to the diocese regarding Christian art and church architecture. In addition, another item on file is a one-man play about Bishop McQuaid, the founder of the Diocese of Rochester, which was produced at an alumni reunion of St. Bernard's Seminary. He also wrote and produced a play about Cardinal Newman for a student presentation.

As I reviewed this body of information, I began to view Father Mac in a more holistic context. Countless people have described him variously as devout, compassionate, and patient; a man of many talents who cheerfully took on new tasks; a thorough researcher; a teacher respected by his students; an able preacher; a priest who was a true follower of Christ; and so forth.

Does this mean that Father Mac had time only for the sublime? Of course not. His quick but kindly sense of humor surely preserved his common sense. Father E. John Townroe, an Anglican priest whom Bishop Fulton J. Sheen engaged in the 1970s as professor of spiritual theology at St. Bernard's Seminary, wrote to my cousin in his later years about his offbeat wit. "I always enjoyed your sudden humorous, often unexpected, remarks. Whether you *intended* to be humorous one judged by the twinkle in your eyes."

For example, Father loved to pose as a whimsical gourmet of desserts. Pies, he contended, are the supreme dessert: "I have never met a pie I didn't like." Apple pie for him was the "king of pies," but to fully deserve that royal title, the individual pie must be made "just so" and eaten only with a piece of sharp cheddar cheese. He claimed also to be a connoisseur of breakfast toast and would reject any spread but marmalade made of bittersweet Seville oranges. For over twenty years, he kept Mrs. Ann Bovenzi, cook at St. Thomas the Apostle rectory in Rochester, supplied with Spanish orange-rind that she was happy to convert, when notified, into yet another batch of the golden preserves.

Some may be shocked to learn that Father Bob had this worldly side. But all is not lost. At the advanced age of ninety-eight, he found it rather easy to compromise a little. He simply ate smaller portions of a tasty pie and spooned out a little less marmalade on his two slices of morning toast. These were not addictions but rather personal preferences.

It was Father Joseph P. Brennan, the fifth rector of St. Bernard's Seminary, who suggested the title of our book, *A Priest Forever*. Psalm 110 is considered a messianic prophecy of the New Testament priesthood of Jesus Christ that would replace the Old Testament priesthood of Moses' brother, Aaron. In verse four, the psalmist solemnly declares, "The Lord has sworn, and he will not repent: You are a priest forever, according to the order of Melchizedek." Naturally, this stirring verse is a key text in the rite of ordination to the Catholic priesthood. There is an ancient Irish prayer, called "St. Patrick's Breastplate," that suggests the relationship of the priestly Apostle of Ireland to his God in poetic terms of balance. Father McNamara was also a realist. This was the prayer Father Bob wanted to use as the framework for this book. More about this later.

As I sat in the congregation at Rochester's St. Thomas the Apostle Church, joining many others in the celebration of Father Bob's ninetieth birthday in 2000, I was struck by what the pastor, Father Robert C. Bradler, said about the nonagenarian. The readings that weekend focused on love of God and love of neighbor. Father McNamara at that time had walking problems, but, as Father Bradler pointed out, "He has maintained daily devotion to prayer and celebrating Mass."

I was filled with admiration for Father Mac's courage. At a time in life when he could easily have slackened his daily routine, he had chosen not to do so and to rely on God's guiding strength. But let us now look at his background.

Born in Corning Hospital in Corning, New York, on November 3, 1910, Robert was the child of Dr. Thomas A. McNamara and Helen Dwyer McNamara. In 1885, his father had married Katherine Dwyer, a Corning schoolteacher, who died in 1897. From Dr. McNamara's first marriage, five children reached maturity: Adrian, Thomas (who became Dr. Thomas L. McNamara), Frances, Evelyn, and Madeline. Katherine's sister, Helen Dwyer, raised them from the time of Katherine's death. In 1906, T. A. McNamara married their beloved "Aunt Nell" Dwyer. Bob was the only child of the second marriage.

From conversations with Father Bob, I sensed that he deeply loved his parents. One of the lights in his world was his father. Their relationship was such that the son, in 2005, published a book about his dad, a typical country physician, *Good Old Doctor Mac: Thomas A. McNamara, Family*

Physician, 1856–1927. He dedicated the book to his brother, Dr. Thomas L. McNamara (father of Susan Marie McNamara-Ten Eyck, my collaborator on this project).

Father Bob also had a deep devotion to his mother. In a letter he wrote to his grand-nephew, Hoytie Bangs (then six years old), he described his own mother hesitantly. It was hard, he said, to articulate what made his Mom so special. Physically, she was a slight person, with the fair skin, ruddy complexion, and reddish-blonde hair she inherited from her father, grocer Thomas Dwyer. Although she participated in various social activities, her favorite place was at home.

From the time Nell McNamara rose in the morning until she went to bed at night, it was said, she would always have the teakettle on the stove. She took very seriously her job as second mother to her sister's children. She was always busy as a parent, housekeeper, and, of course, superlative cook.

Another reason people loved Bob's mother was her smiling disposition. She was, however, deeper than a smile. She loved God, learned patience and wisdom from him, and utilized the gift he had given her of heartening people by her own words and example. Like her sister Kate, she was a woman people would turn to in moments of trouble.

Bob attended St. Mary's parish school from 1916 to 1924. Then he switched to Corning Free Academy, a superior public high school (1924-1928). The college that he chose was at Georgetown University in Washington, D.C. (1928-1932), where he majored in English literature. He spent the year 1932-33 at Harvard University earning a master of arts degree, also in English literature. Upon completion of these literary studies, he embarked (to the surprise of even his family) on a future in the Catholic diocesan priesthood. When he was 14, he told me, he had "heard a voice" informing him, "You will, of course, be a priest." This he considered "not a command, but a grace," and he accepted it as a private communication – probably the only mystical experience of his life. In the fall of 1933, he left Corning for Rome, Italy, to begin four years of theological studies.

Father Bob's "secret": "I first informed my family of my vocation in a letter to my mother from Cambridge, Massachusetts, dated early in the week of Sunday, November 6, 1932. She replied with a special delivery letter at the end of the same week. A single sentence of it summarizes her tender reaction: 'If God really called my son to serve him, I rejoice; but I feel so unworthy of such a blessing.'"

Bob McNamara became Father McNamara with his priestly ordination in the beautiful little Roman chapel of the North American College on December 8, 1936, the feast of the Immaculate Conception of the Blessed Virgin Mary. He was happy to have his mother present that day, as well as his brother Dr. Thomas L. McNamara; his sister Madeline; and his niece, fifteen-year-old Katherine Van Wagner, a daughter of his married sister Evelyn McNamara (Mrs. Harry F. Van Wagner).

Priests ordained in Rome are allowed to say three "first Masses" (that is, three successive Masses with certain special ceremonies). He offered his initial Mass in the Basilica of St. Mary Major at the altar of the Crib of Bethlehem. His second Mass was at the church of Santa Croce, with its precious relics of Christ's Passion. For the site of his third Mass, he chose the chapel of a home for the elderly in the Trastevere section of Rome. The symbolism of his choices was this: the first Mass honored the Incarnation, the second Mass honored the Redemption, and the third Mass honored the Mystical Body of Christ (that is, all the faithful united in a heavenly body with Jesus himself as their Head).

When he returned from Rome in August of 1937, Father Bob sang his first Solemn High Mass in his home church of St. Mary's in Corning. Parishioners, friends, and relatives filled the church on Sunday, August 15, for a service rich in the Roman Catholic liturgical tradition. Delivering the homily that morning, Monsignor Walter J. Lee of Geneva described the priesthood as a call to the service of God's people, concluding with this message to the celebrant. "Father McNamara, you are the son of the late Dr. Thomas A. McNamara, a man greatly loved in this community. He devoted his efforts toward the physical assistance of mankind, and you, for the remainder of your life, will devote your efforts toward the salvation of souls." (It was an interesting parallel: father and son were both healers.)

A few days later the new priest received his first assignment, assistant pastor of St. Francis Xavier Church in Rochester, NY. Although he was to live at St. Francis rectory, most of his work would be to serve the Italian families at the Chapel of the Annunciation, one of two Italian missions entrusted to Father George Weinmann, pastor of St. Francis Xavier. It was assumed that after four years in Italy he would know enough Italian to preach and hear confessions. Actually, he was still a learner in Italian, although the gracious parishioners appreciated his efforts to speak their beautiful tongue.

Father Bob would eventually speak Italian well enough to teach it, but he was spared further pressure by an unexpected transfer in June 1939 to the post of associate editor of the diocesan newspaper, the *Catholic Courier Journal.* His residence was also changed to St. Ann's Home for the Aged, founded by Bishop McQuaid in 1906. With the residence went the duties of chaplain of the home. He offered his first Mass there on July 11, 1939.

Transfer to St. Ann's would seem to be almost prophetic. The home then stood on its original site, 1971 Lake Avenue, just a piece down the road from St. Bernard's Theological Seminary (2260 Lake Avenue) although on the other side of the street. He was scarcely settled at St. Ann's when he found himself reassigned to St. Bernard's, a diocesan/interdiocesan graduate school for priests, as a member of the faculty. Here is what happened. Father Frederick J. Zwierlein, D.Sc.M.H. (Louvain), the distinguished Rochesterian who had taught Church history at St. Bernard's for many years, decided just then to retire. Whom did Bishop James E. Kearney name to succeed him?

Father Bob!

The new professor had a licentiate (master's degree) in theology, which qualified him to teach in a Catholic seminary; he had, as we have seen, a master's degree in English literature; but he had neither a degree nor even much schooling in history. Embarrassing! Fortunately, the seminary rector, Monsignor John Francis Goggin, proposed an acceptable arrangement. Father Bob would teach Church history for a few years "experimentally." Then he could go to a university, on leave for doctoral studies.

Actually, the young professor became so engrossed in his new field of study that he was happy to learn Church history "in the saddle." World War II hampered graduate studies in general, and in the postwar period obligations towards his family made going back to school impracticable. The seminary rector never raised the issue of the postponed degree again, nor did Father McNamara; but he did lament his lack of rigorous historical training. "I guess God did not want me to earn a doctorate in history," he has said, "and rightly so. I would probably have become a total snob."

Father Bob's retirement in 1981 coincided with the official closing of St. Bernard's undergraduate department because of diminishing vocations. At the final commencement, the faculty bestowed on him an honorary D.D. (Doctor of Divinity) degree – a gesture he deeply appreciated. Meanwhile, however, he had come to realize that his literary studies had not been wasted. They had taught him how to research and to write not only literature but history. In 1984, Rochester's St. John Fisher College would vote to confer on him yet another honorary doctorate, the L.H.D. (Doctor of Humane Letters). Reviewers of his centennial history, *The Diocese of Rochester 1868-1968,* had referred to the author's skill as both scholar and writer. Father Thomas T. McAvoy, C.S.C., professor of history at Notre Dame University, even called him "one of the best historical craftsmen of American Catholicism." Fisher College, it seems, had awarded the perfect kudos!

During those 43 years he had risen to the rank of Full Professor of Church History. In addition to history, he taught, at various times, patrology, liturgy, and Italian. In the spring semesters of 1972 and 1976, he commuted weekly to Toronto as Visiting Professor of U. S. Catholic History in the Toronto School of Theology. Meanwhile he was kept busy writing and publishing several books and assorted articles on religious history, local history, secular history, and non-history, thus acquiring a much wider audience than just his seminarians.

Looking back upon his teaching career, I wondered whether God had intentionally steered Father Bob to St. Bernard's Seminary so that from this centralized address he could easily steer others, both seminarians and externs, along the path to God. In one of his sermons I found at least a partial answer.

Although not a parish priest after 1939, my cousin was happy to be a weekend assistant at St. Salome's Church for 39 years. He carefully preserved the sermons he preached there. One sermon in particular caught my attention. Here he spoke of the "light of the world." "God the Father is the creator of physical light in the world," he said. "God the Son is the spiritual light of the world. ... Our duty is to reflect in our own lives the light which is Christ. And we do this by living according to his law."

"When we live by Christ's law," he explained, "we share our bread with the hungry, shelter the oppressed and homeless, clothe the naked, and do not turn our back on our own."

After his retirement in 1981, Father Bob moved to St. Thomas the Apostle rectory. He kept himself busy with his writings and priestly duties, helping with Masses, confessions, and sacraments. When the Adoration Chapel opened, he took on the task of opening and closing the chapel daily. On April 8, 2002, he moved to the McAuley Residence at the Sisters of Mercy Motherhouse, where he was kept busy and received much loving care until his death.

I began to see how radiant Father Bob himself had been in the lives of so many other people, myself included. He was advising everybody to imitate the behavior of Jesus that St. Paul had recommended to the Corinthians. "Be imitators of me, as I am of Christ" (1 Cor. 11:1). Incidentally, Cardinal John Henry Newman asked for that same favor when he prayed, "Help me, Lord, to spread your fragrance wherever I go; let me preach without preaching, not by words but by example." St. Patrick of Ireland, as early as the fifth century, seems also to have advocated this "imitation of Christ" when he implored, "And may I follow the way of God." (Such a desire is attributed to St. Patrick in the "Breastplate of St. Patrick," an ecstatic Morning Prayer. Although the saint himself may not have been the author of the "Breastplate," the prayer does seem to express his concept of the priest as "another Christ.")

Here, then, is a brief sketch of Father McNamara's life. Now we must hurry on to evaluate not only our personal experiences of his words and deeds, but also the testimony of a cloud of other witnesses (Heb.12:1) who have considered him exemplary.

CHAPTER TWO

Summon the Witnesses!

On, now, with our project: to refute the charge made by "the foolish" (1 Pet. 2:15), that Catholic priests today are "rascals." How? By recounting the commendable life of *just one* American Catholic priest whom good people consider model. One should be enough!

If we had asked a committee of lay Catholic men and women to pick that priest, they would doubtless have looked first to one of the many present-day American pastors, zealous and even heroic. We have decided, however, to choose a priest who was a seminary professor. Those are the real priest-makers! Theirs is an awesome double duty: to train seminarians to be both apostles and shepherds. Apostles, ready to pass on *intact* the revelation of Jesus Christ. Shepherds, ready to *die*, if need be, for the sheep (John 10:14-15).

We have chosen as our subject Father Robert Francis McNamara. A native of Corning, New York, in the Southern Tier in the Diocese of Rochester, he resided and taught Church history at St. Bernard's Seminary, Rochester, from 1939 to 1981. While there, he had little contact with the city of Rochester around him. But inside the seminary walls he spent himself generously in the formation of other "priests forever."

When we "summoned the witnesses" to Father Bob's notable life and works, we naturally focused on the mostly local persons and groups with whom he had the closest connection, especially the seminary students and his own relatives. Let me tell you first about the well-remembered Christmas custom he established just for Church History One.

Father Mac was an inventive teacher, always ready to use appropriate new techniques to maintain interest during his classes. For example, early in his general Church history course for the "new men" of First Philosophy (the junior year of college), he introduced a special pre-Christmas feature at the last class session before the holidays. Father John T. Reif (Rochester Diocese, class of 1965) has kindly volunteered to record his own recollections of that perennial event when he himself was a newcomer. He labels the memo "Flashback 1959: St. Bernard's Seminary, Rochester, New York."

"Our ordination class of 1965 numbered about forty-five. On a mid-December morning, we are seated in a long rectangular lecture hall. The Professor of Church History is seated at the desk before us. On this particular December morning, however, he is not teaching! Instead he is opening Christmas gifts – but they are not for *him*. The gifts are for children either hospitalized or among the city's impoverished. At some point between this December morning and Christmas morning itself, our Church History Professor will arrange for the presents to reach their destination. The children will receive the wind-up toys, etc., but the Christ-like Santa – alias Father McNamara – will perhaps be the happiest of all.

"How many years old was this tradition? I have no idea. I do know, however, that it took place in First Philosophy, throughout our six years at St. Bernard's. My guess is that it predated our time and went on after our time. [3] Certainly, one thing stands out from the memory of this pre-Christmas ritual: the dancing eyes of Father McNamara anticipating the joys of the children come Christmas time.

---

[3] Father Bob recalled: "I may have started the practice as early as 1939, but it was probably a few years later. I continued it until 1968. In that year our "Philosophers" (juniors and seniors in college) transferred to St. John Fisher College. After that I taught only students in the four years of theology. I passed the toys over to the Trinitarian Sisters who were then working in Rochester's inner city. Our pre-Christmas "inspection of the gifts" seemed to please; thus it became a little parable on Christmas charity. In my own remarks, I usually added the charming medieval story, 'How the Animals Went to Bethlehem.'"

"I believe that this yearly event truly spoke to the essence of who this beloved man was: Christ-like, scholarly, perceptive, humble, and humorous. Day after day and through the years, he brought to his students what he also brought to his church congregations and his readers: genuine Catholic-Christian holiness and wisdom, all wrapped up in the wonder of a child's expression on Christmas morning. Father McNamara lived the words of Jesus: 'Whoever does not accept the kingdom of God like a child will not enter it' (Mark 10:15)."

Now, if Father Reif's class of 1965 numbered about forty-five in 1959, that means that not only he but some forty other students were witnesses to Father Mac's annual "toy day." Multiply forty-five by the number of years the practice continued, and your count of enchanted seminary witnesses mounts to more than a thousand! Its simplicity touched them deeply.

Many of the priests whom Father Bob taught as seminarians still have vivid memories of his classes, especially his lively lectures on Christian history and religious art. "I shall never forget Father McNamara's Christian Art lectures in the *aula* [auditorium] of St. Bernard's Seminary," says Father Richard Beligotti (Rochester, class of 1968). "I looked forward to them – especially the slides that 'Father Bobby' collected over the years to illustrate the great artistic treasury of our Catholic faith. ... It is because of him that I now cherish so much of our Catholic cultural heritage."

Of Father Bob's character, Father Richard continues, "He was a fine role model as a humble, gentle, patient priest with a fine sense of humor. He was always encouraging his students, and ever respectful of our particular gifts. He was positive in his outlook and filled with hope – hope for us and for the Church. He is to me an example of strong, persevering faith." ("Bobby," of course, was the nickname the students gave to Father McNamara. He said he never knew that! What esprit de corps those seminarians had!)

Many of his seminary students learned of Father Bob's reputation as a teacher when they continued on to further studies. Father Robert C. MacNamara (Rochester, class of 1951) affirms "the great value and weight his Church history classes had in academic credit toward post-graduate degrees in non-theological programs." This Father MacNamara (not related to my cousin but often confused with him) also recalls that the Professor of Church History put his students at ease when it was time for their oral Latin canonical exams, "the formal questioning of our preparedness. He was the soul of kindness to men 'threatened' by other interrogators on the faculty."

This might be the best place to quote the definition of Father Bob offered by Father Thomas Hoctor (Rochester, class of 1957): "He was our hero. He would *speak* with the students, and the students could tease him. He was not a distant person."

One of the students whom Father Bob taught at St. Bernard's Seminary was Matthew H. Clark (Albany, class of 1963), now bishop emeritus of Rochester. Bishop Clark met Father Bob in 1957 and studied Church history for two years at St. Bernard's prior to his theological studies in Rome. As Bishop Clark says in his foreword to this book, he found Father Bob "committed to both his subjects and his students," and personally "very gracious and kind."

Another longtime friend, Monsignor J. Emmett Murphy (Rochester, class of 1939) met Father Bob in 1935 when he began his studies at the Gregorian University with residence at the North American College in Rome. It was customary for an upper classman from the same diocese to take a new man under his wing and show him the "Roman ropes." Father Bob mentored the Rochester newcomer Emmett Murphy and the two became fast friends. Monsignor Murphy never forgot Father Bob's kindness, a quality he called the outstanding feature of his mentor's life.

Murphy and McNamara crossed paths again in 1946 when the Monsignor was added to the faculty of St. Bernard's Seminary. He soon perceived that Father Bob was "beloved by the students. He inspired them by his deep piety and faithfulness to duty. ... He is a great, kindly, holy priest," Monsignor said, "a true and happy follower of Christ."

Father Joseph A. Hart (Rochester, class of 1972), now a vicar general of the Rochester Diocese, is another priest whom Father Bob taught at the seminary. As a student, Father Hart was impressed by the depth of knowledge and attention to detail that Father Bob displayed. Looking back on those days, he lists four attributes to describe Father Bob as a teacher: his great love of the Church; his willingness to take on extra work; his patience with students; and the great care he took to be charitable in all things.

Father Frank Lioi (Rochester, class of 1967), who would later serve as the last rector of St. Bernard's, also looks back fondly on his studies there with Father Bob. In 1989, on the occasion of Father Mac's golden jubilee as a teacher, Father Lioi wrote to him: "It is only as I get older that I realize the tremendous amount of knowledge that you imparted to us as students of St. Bernard's Seminary. What were at one time only facts and dates have become, over the years, tangible realities and vivid experiences. I thank you for planting the seeds of an appreciation of history and art which are still coming to fruition."

Another comment by Father Mac: He thanks Father Lioi for *his* thanks. "I am sure any teacher would be happy to learn that his disciples have taken to heart at least some of the good things he has taught them. I doubt that I have ever given adequate thanks to my own wonderful teachers for the wisdom they tried to impart to me." What teacher, indeed, could ask for a higher tribute than to see his influence for good with his students resonate through the years?

The remainder of this chapter will feature the testimony of other principal witnesses: his relatives, students, associates, priests, religious, and scholars. We will also quote from some of the professor's own self-revealing sermons and public statements.

On the fiftieth anniversary of his ordination in 1986, Father Bob took the occasion of a luncheon at St. Thomas the Apostle rectory to speak briefly about the changes he had seen during his five decades as a priest. Sometimes it had seemed that the Church was traveling calm waters. At other times – particularly during his second twenty-five years – it had seemed that the Church was riding a tempest. He reminded his listeners that Jesus never promised that life on this earth would be smooth sailing. What he did promise was to be with us always until the end of time, a richer gift. Like the Apostles whose boat was caught in that storm at sea, we have no reason to be afraid. As Jesus said to them after he had rebuked the wind and calmed the water, "Why are you terrified? Do you not yet have faith?" (Mark 4:40)

For the past forty-nine years, Father Bob then said, he had been instructing people to continue strong in faith. That was still his message on his golden jubilee in 1986. He offered the following simple advice: "Don't ever miss your daily prayers; go to confession individually, and frequently; be faithful about attending Sunday Mass (and go to weekday Mass, too, as you can). Don't forget voluntary acts of self-denial. And especially remember to confirm your faith each day by an Act of Faith; or by reciting the Creeds (Nicene and Apostle's); or at least say to Jesus: 'I do believe. Help my unbelief' (Mark 9:24)." Father Bob concluded his remarks with a little Italian prayer to Mary that he learned in Rome: "Vergine Immacolata aiutateci" (Spotless Virgin and your dear Son, bless and keep us every one). ("Add this to your own aspirations if you like," he told me. "There's no copyright!")

Nineteen years later, when we were talking about this book, Father Bob again spoke about the epoch of his priesthood. It had been full of turmoil, he said, in both the secular world and the Church. The world has suffered many wars, and the Church, too, has endured many conflicts and challenges to faith.

So how has Father Bob dealt with all these adversities? As Christ himself would say: "Through my trust in God the Father." When Father William Graf once asked him about handling trials, Father Bob's witty but wise response was, "I keep one foot firmly planted in the past and one in the present, and my eyes on the future."

During his thirty-nine years as a weekend priest at St. Salome's in Irondequoit, Father Mac preached almost every Sunday. Later in life he found, to his surprise, that many of the parishioners still have vivid recollections of his sermons. "His homilies were teaching tools," says Father Conrad Sundholm (Rochester, class of 1955), who had been one of Father's altar boys at St. Salome's. "We were always able to learn something from his preaching."

Father Joseph Hart has observed that when priests preach they disclose themselves and their spirituality – their relationship with God. Because of this, he says, people will always be attracted to a good preacher – like Father Bob – who helps them consider their own rapport with God. A good illustration, perhaps, is this excerpt from his homily given at the 1981 wedding of Andrea Ciaccio and Dr. James Bracikowski:

"The greatest key to a good marriage is love. How God loves married couples! Does he not share with them his work of creation as they bring new lives into the world? Does he not share with them his work of redemption, too: are they not the first to preach salvation to their own little ones? . . . What is more beautiful than a home where parents dedicated in faith, hope, and love pass on these virtues to their children? . . . St. Paul says to couples: 'Let everyone see that you are interested only in the highest ideals.' Families that exemplify love of God and neighbor are not only honorable among Americans; they are the very foundation of our American society. . . .

"Finally, I speak to all the other married couples here. Take this beautiful occasion to renew to each other your own commitment to each other in faith and hope and love: perhaps by a glance, or a squeeze of the hand, or at the sign of peace, a kiss.

"And I pray God in the words of Pope John Paul II: 'Grant that your grace may guide the thoughts and actions of husbands and wives for the good of their families and all the families of the world'."

There were other ways in which Father Bob's presence at St. Salome's was vividly felt and the promptings of the Spirit in his life were evident. Mary Napoleon, a member of the parish, will never forget the morning of Sunday, May 17, 1952, when Father Bob ran out of the church to anoint David Vicart, a seven-year-old who had been gravely injured while playing on heavy road-building equipment parked just outside. Without stopping to change from his vestments, he rushed to the spot and knelt in the dirt, praying over the child. That image, Mary says, sums up Father Bob for her: always there when needed. Appropriately, it was also he who celebrated little David's sad memorial Mass a few days later.

Ms. Napoleon also recalled an amusing story about Father Bob and some of her relatives. Her aunt and uncle came over from Italy one summer to visit them. They spoke no English, and when they wished to go to confession they didn't imagine there would be a priest in Rochester who could understand them. Mary introduced them to Father Bob and explained the situation. Her aunt and uncle were surprised to meet an

Irish-American priest in the Diocese of Rochester who spoke Italian and regularly heard Italian confessions.

Father Bob's views about radiating Christ in one's life are also well illustrated in this excerpt from the baccalaureate sermon he delivered at his Washington, D.C., alma mater, Georgetown University. He gave the graduates good advice at that time, based on the Catholic conviction that God grants to all human beings certain leadership talents that he expects them to use for the benefit of both their Creator and their neighbor:

"The 1957 graduate who is to become a priest -- and there are nearly always some -- will find many such passages [in Scripture], but perhaps the most memorable of them is 'As the Father has sent me, so I send you' (John 20:22). The 1957 graduate who is to practice medicine is also called to a Christ-like life; for it can be said of him, in a certain sense, as it was said of Christ, 'power came forth from him and he healed them all' (Luke 6:19).

"Let those who become lawyers or lawmakers take as their own Christ's declaration: 'Do not think that I have come to abolish the Law or the Prophets. I have come not to abolish but to fulfill' (Matt 5:17). Let those who enter Foreign Service become, in foreign lands, a mirror of their own nation, guided by Christ's beatitude: 'Blessed are the peacemakers, for they will be called children of God' (Matt 5:9). Will you be a soldier? Then remember how Our Lord admired the soldier who assured him: 'I, too, am a person subject to authority' (Matt 8:9). Will you be a sailor or a Marine? Then remember how safe was the Galilean ship when it had aboard the Christ 'whom even the winds and the sea obey' (Matt 8:27). Will you engage in business? Then remember that Christ in parable praised the merchants and bankers who were enterprising, and condemned only the shiftless man as a 'wicked, lazy servant' (Mt. 25: 14-30).

"What the world needs today is good leadership: good leadership in the professions, in government, in business, in the community. By your talents and by your training, you, the graduates of 1957, are called upon to exercise this leadership: perhaps in a major way, perhaps in a minor way – no matter.

To prepare yourselves for this leadership, whether in your own profession or in society at large, be guided by sound ideals, and imitate the heroes who in their own lives have exemplified those sound ideals. And the ultimate norm of ideals is the teachings of Christ, just as the ultimate norm of heroism is the heroism of Christ. If you follow this program faithfully, you will grow, as St. Paul promised, 'to mature manhood, to the extent of the full stature of Christ' (Ephesians 4:13).

"Do not be afraid to aspire to great things, Class of 1957. And may God be with you!"

In charming contrast to his scholarly abilities, Father Bob always had a delightful way of communicating with children. He treated them with gentle respect. His niece Margot Sheeran Rooney gave us this good illustration.

"I was about four or five and Uncle Bob had come to stay with us for a day or two. One morning, he was walking around the house very deep in thought, as he was saying his morning prayers. He was actually reading from a book (probably his Missal). [4] Well, I decided that I could do the same and I started to follow him, reading also – but my book was a comic book. When my parents saw me, they tried to get my attention to stop without interrupting Uncle Bob, but the more they tried the funnier I thought it was. The scene finally ended when Uncle Bob concluded his prayers and said to me with a twinkle, 'I am finished. Are you?'"

To his friends – many of whom he knew for decades – Father Bob showed a kindly affection. Monsignor Gerry Krieg, a former student of Father Bob's at the seminary, later came to know him also as a close friend when both were serving at St. Salome's Parish. Monsignor Krieg began to see the man who had been his teacher through the eyes of the parishioners, who loved him for his presence as a priest among them. The two developed an enduring friendship that stretched across the years into

---

[4] Father Bob clarified: "It would have been the Breviary, from which priests pray daily."

their retirements. Father Bob "deepened my own sense of worth, and that is the way friendships should be," Monsignor Krieg says. We gave one another insight into our own and each other's self-worth." Summarizing what many feel about Father Bob, he concludes, "Of all the world's values, the ultimate value is a person who images divinity to others."

In May 2005, the feast of the Body and Blood of Christ coincided with the Memorial Day weekend. That Monday, I forced myself to take on the work of cleaning out my home office. After some time at that task, I paused in front of the filing cabinet, unhappy and annoyed. This was a holiday, I thought, as well as a beautiful day, and here I was indoors toiling at work that was so tedious! But while I was enjoying this self-pity, my thoughts turned to Father Bob the writer. He certainly did a great deal of sorting out and organizing material for the many books and articles he wrote. With Father Bob in mind, I began to understand that no task is complete until all the pieces, big and little, have been put in their proper places – as in a picture puzzle!

As I reflected on this, I recalled that many people have spoken with admiration about Father Bob's attention to detail. Father Conrad Sundholm praises his impressive breadth of knowledge, describing him as a man who attended carefully to detail and took on "jobs that no one else wanted." One of those jobs was arranging for the sacramental records of all the parishes in the Diocese of Rochester to be put on microfilm – a project of immeasurable value to genealogists and historians. Father Thomas Hoctor told me, too, that Father Bob was largely responsible for initiating the detailed process through which the buildings of St. Bernard's Seminary were given historic landmark status.

Monsignor Emmett Murphy pointed to the dedication with which Father Bob wrote his history of their Roman alma mater, the North American College. It took Father Bob thirteen years to complete that task, which included travel to various American dioceses and churches, as well as to Rome itself. While this was not the first book written about the Pontifical North American College, it remains the most complete history of that institution's first centenary.

Rome's Jesuit periodical *La Civiltà Cattolica* called this hefty volume a "masterly study." An American Jesuit explained its merits in greater detail in an unpublished review: "You've done more in this work than recount the history of a single institution," wrote Father Edward B. Bunn, S.J., president of Georgetown University, to Father Bob after reading a copy of *The American College in Rome*. "You've caught also and tied into your story the spirit of an age – its struggles and triumphs, its strengths and weaknesses – and you've succeeded in giving background and perspective to many of the problems of our own day …. And alongside the clarity and vision of the historian, you have retained the sympathy of the humanist, with admiration for the fine qualities of the personages who walk through your pages, and a tolerant attitude – often with a chuckle – for human weakness and foibles. In a word, it is a grand book, not only for those who have attended the college and hold it in loving remembrance, but for all of us who love and cherish Rome and all it stands for, in secular history and religious tradition."

For his intense effort to write this book Father Bob was chosen the first recipient of the prestigious Founders' Medal of the Pontifical North American College. In establishing this award, the Board of Governors of the college unanimously singled out Father Bob as a priest and scholar whose name is virtually synonymous with his Roman alma mater. The citation that accompanied the gold medal reads as follows:

"In his fifty-four years of priesthood our honoree has labored in parish work, youth ministry and journalism. He has been the diocese's archivist since 1976, and for over forty years served as Professor of Church History in its seminary. He has recorded the story of the historical American Church in many scholarly articles. His books include a history of his diocese and a [historical] complete study on [American] Catholic Sunday Preaching.

"Ordained from the Pontifical North American College Class of 1937, he views his centennial history, *The American College in Rome, 1855-1955*, as his gift of gratitude to the Seminary which nourished, strengthened, and formed him. To this day that work survives as a monument to his scholarship, to his love of Alma Mater, and to the noble accomplishments of the College and her sons during a century of change and growth in Church and Nation. His influence upon priests and upon Church history is beyond measure. His steadfast and undaunted love for the College sets a standard to which all her alumni might aspire. Uniquely, he has rendered extraordinary service to our College. The Board of Governors is therefore pleased, in the name of the Pontifical North American College, to award the first Founders' Medal to FATHER ROBERT FRANCIS McNAMARA of the Diocese of Rochester.

"Given in Washington, D. C., June 12, 1990, during the One Hundred First Annual Meeting of the Alumni Association of the North American College."

(Signed) + James Cardinal Hickey
Chairman, Board of Governors

In 2011, Cardinal (then Archbishop) Timothy Dolan of New York wrote:

"While I was a graduate student in Church history at the Catholic University of America, the revered professor of American Catholic history, Monsignor John Tracy Ellis, told us that, in general, histories of seminaries were hardly worth the read. The only exception, he quickly added, was *The American College in Rome*, by Robert McNamara.

"So, of course, I read it … and re-read it. Not only that, but when I became rector of that college, I encouraged the seminarians to read it, and made sure it had a prominent place on the library's reference shelf.

"I even looked into its re-print -- with an update -- since his book only goes up to the opening of the new college in 1953 -- a task I have yet to give up on.

"In letters, phone conversations, and visits with Father McNamara, I have found him not only a first-class historian, but a splendid priest, who exudes the virtues his beloved North American College attempts to impart."

Given his respect for language and fine attention to detail, it is easy to understand why Rochester archivist and historian Kathleen Urbanic should declare Father Bob "the world's best proofreader. He never missed a thing!"

My cousin often said that when he saw "bits of history" that needed to be written up for the record, he usually did it himself. (He *usually* had most of the information, anyhow!) A case in point was his decision to write the biography of his father, Dr. Thomas A. McNamara. His original thought was to provide an account of his dad's medical and civic life for family members who had never known the doctor. After distributing mimeographed copies of the first draft to Doctor Mac's descendants, he decided to rewrite the story for a wider circulation. This became a labor of love on which he worked off-and-on for almost twenty years. The final product, *Good Old Doctor Mac: Thomas A. McNamara, Family Physician, 1856-1921,* was published in 2004. It is the portrait of a typical small-town physician practicing in western New York from 1882 to 1927. As the author says of his parent in the preface: "He was no major figure in either national or medical annals; but he did typify the conscientious medic of the era, a man of professional integrity and civic pride."

"This book," said William Treichler in his *Crooked Lake Review* (Hammondsport, New York), "is the success story of a first-generation rural Irish-American immigrant family: its Americanization, its trials, its triumphs." (A good summary of an affectionate little volume!)

Senior priests of the Diocese of Rochester have long spoken well of Father Mac's style of historical writing. The late Father Joseph P. Brennan did not live to see the publication of this book which owes its title largely to him. But again and again he used to comment on Father Bob's readability. Another local priest who spoke well of this readability was Rochester's heroic bemedalled World War II chaplain, Father Elmer Heindl. "Father Bob," he said, "has never tried to rewrite history. He has always tried to explain history in the context of the times.... He has a talent for making history come alive, of explaining things past in a way that is relevant to the present." Father Sebastian Falcone, a former professor of sacred scripture and dean of studies at St. Bernard's Seminary, takes a scholar's interest in the techniques of historical narrative as demonstrated by Father McNamara. He notes that the former history professor had "a special love for the total history of the Church. He dug deeply into the background of topics.... He ... always worked to give the information he shared a permanent quality. But not only did he love history, he loved the English tongue. Committed to correctness in the use of the spoken and written word, he recognized the importance of good language in pastoral communication." Father Sebastian, himself a skilled preacher and connoisseur of words, nodded approvingly as he said of our historian, "He constantly checked dictionaries and encyclopedias to verify origins and the historical meanings of words."

At this point, after listening to many priests about their "Father Bob" memories, I wondered whether he had had any assignments with the nuns who taught at St. Salome or St. Thomas the Apostle schools. "Oh, yes," he replied, "I saw much of the Sisters of Mercy who taught in both schools, but I had no special assignment to them. Remember I was only a 'weekender.' My contacts were generally priestly ones: celebrating Mass, hearing confessions, giving spiritual direction and the like."

Sister Roberta Rodenhouse, R.S.M., lived at both convents over the years. She wrote a tribute when she was living at St. Thomas the Apostle convent and Father Bob was resident in its rectory. Here she praised "his kindness to the Sisters: each Saturday morning for many years, he said Mass in the convent chapel, continuing to do so even when physical infirmity no longer allowed him to stand at the altar during the service. When the Sisters moved from the convent building to a nearby house, they converted an enclosed porch into a chapel where Father Bob continued to say a weekly Mass for them." Sister Roberta also came to know another side of Father Bob when he served as her spiritual director. "He was always there when you needed him," she says. "He was a wonderful counselor, a wonderful listener."

Dr. Joseph G. Kelly, a retired professor of religious studies at Nazareth College who knew Father Mac for many years, considered him both friend and mentor. When Dr. Kelly became a member of the faculty of St. Bernard's Seminary (1970 – 1981), he gained a deeper appreciation of the priest's fine sense of collegiality. Prior to Joe's visit to Israel in 1977, Father Bob slipped him an envelope with instructions not to open it until he was en route to the Holy Land. Dutifully following these instructions, Dr. Kelly discovered that the envelope contained Israeli currency, with a note that it was to be used to pay the "temple tax" – as pilgrims visiting Jerusalem for the first time were accustomed to do in Old Testament times.

In recent years, Dr. Kelly also enjoyed the custom of serving his long-time friend and teacher at Masses celebrated on his two special days: his birthday on November 3, and his anniversary of ordination on December 8.

While Father Bob was widely regarded for his research and writing skills, he also proved himself equally skillful at procuring material that needed to be saved. In 1976, he was appointed archivist for the Rochester Diocese, and began the challenging work of organizing and preserving the diocese's historical documents, photographs, and artifacts. "He *saved* the history of the diocese," says Father William Graf, his former student and longtime collaborator. "Father Bob made sure that things were collected!" Given a permanent home in the diocesan Pastoral Center in 1989, the archives include the Bishop Fulton Sheen Collection, among countless other records of Catholicism in Rochester. No one radiated more pleasure on the day the archives office was dedicated than Father Bob, whose long vision had made the Rochester archives a reality.

As archivist, Father Bob spent himself beyond the call of duty for researchers and scholars. Many will attest that he not only furnished information from the diocesan holdings, but also provided it in rich historical context. Kathleen Urbanic is one researcher who, by her own admission, will be forever in his debt. "I met Father Bob in 1983, when I was gathering information for a history of Rochester's Polish community. My research led me to the diocesan archives, where I hoped to look at documents relating to the upheaval surrounding the formation of the Polish National Catholic parish of St. Casimir. When Father Bob provided me with copies of Bishop McQuaid's correspondence relating to St. Casimir's, I felt as if he were giving me gold. More than that, he took me – a fledgling researcher naïve enough to feel I could write a book – under his wing and helped me understand the story of St. Casimir's Parish in the context of American Catholic Church history, immigration history, and local history. When I asked him to read the chapter of my book relating to St. Casimir's, he graciously offered to review the whole manuscript. Father Bob gently guided my project from that point forward, and I am proud to say that the final product (*Shoulder to Shoulder: Polish Americans in Rochester, NY*) bears the mark of his scholarship."

Archivist McNamara said he looked back with special pleasure on his contacts with four American historians whom he assisted in the preparation of their books: Patrick W. Carey (*People, Priests and Prelates: Ecclesiastical Democracy and the Tensions of Trusteeism,* Notre Dame University Press, 1989); Kathleen L. Riley (*Fulton J. Sheen: An American Catholic Response to the Twentieth* Century, Alba House Press, 2004); Richard Gribble, C.S.C. (*An Archbishop for the People: The Life of Edward J. Hanna,* Paulist Press, 2006); Leonard R. Riforgiato (*The Life and Times of John Timon: First Bishop of Buffalo, NY,* Dennis A. Castillo, editor. Edwin Mellen Press, Lewiston, NY, 2006). Willingness to share the expanse of his knowledge with others also made Father Bob an essential resource for local journalists like Michael Latona. "In my many years with the *Catholic Courier,* I have benefited greatly from the vast knowledge of Father McNamara," he says. "Father Bob has not only written stories for our newspaper, but has given excellent interviews.... What comes across is his obvious love of writing history, a subject not always easy to present in a winning fashion. Yet in bringing this liveliness to his narrative, he refuses to compromise truth. As a journalist, I have deep respect for such an ethical code."

"Father Bob saw himself as a collector of stories," Father William Graf observes. "He had a wide acquaintance with history, music, and the fine arts. To him, every question and every inquiry was important. . . . He was a gentleman and a scholar, and always the priest. He brought the best of intellectual life to the priesthood and the Church. He certainly opened new worlds to his seminarians."

As I reflected on Father Bob, I gained an even deeper regard for him. He made many quiet contributions as a writer, historian, and archivist, and this work had a rather surprising impact, ready as he always was to offer others the benefit of his own experience. Many people, I imagine, would consider historical research dull and tedious. Father Bob found it a joyous incentive to inform and inspire those who are studying our human past. Is it time, perhaps, to give his efforts some public recognition?

We summon the witnesses!

Witness Father Robert C. MacNamara, who is a Rochester priest and St. Bernard's alumnus and has good-naturedly endured being mistaken for Father Bob over the years, cites many comic examples of the confusion with his professional namesake. "As a very young priest (1951), I began to receive mail and phone calls all destined for him. . . . At times I received episcopal invitations from the North American College in Rome, wedding invitations, Christmas cards, legal notices and bills! All meant for him. When I was in Elmira and assigned to a Corning pastorate in 1983, the confusion only deepened as many Corningites thought that their native son was returning to the Crystal City. I learned in those days about 'my' [his] father as people recalled Dr. McNamara for me. Through all those years, phone calls have reached me about some historical nicety, and I have tried politely to direct inquiries to 'the other Bob' . . . . When I attended Catholic University to take courses in Church history, the professor-colleagues of Father Bob were perplexed to learn that he was coming there. The eminent historical scholar John Tracy Ellis was visibly disappointed when I appeared."

While it could be expected that Father Bob would be well regarded within scholarly circles and in the brotherhood of priests, others also hold him in high esteem, especially parishioners from St. Salome's. Witness Jeanne Marie Bello, who grew up in St. Salome's Parish, speaks of how happy she used to feel whenever Father Bob came to visit her family and enjoy her mother's homemade kidney stew. "When Father Bob would come into our home," she says, "it was like Christ himself coming in."

When Jeanne Marie was a teenager, her family experienced serious difficulties and her parents divorced. During that painful time, Father Bob's presence brought her comfort and a sense of security. "Our father may have left our family," she says, "but Father Bob entered, and God gave us the best in both a spiritual and secular father." After Jeanne Marie married, she stayed in close contact with Father Bob. He baptized her two boys, played games with them, and hid Easter eggs for them to discover. "Father Bob always had a sparkle in his eye. No matter who else might be visiting us, they always felt at home with him. He appreciated the joys – as well as the struggles – of everyday life."

I'm certain the reader has noticed that all of the witnesses are my cousin's brother priests of the American Catholic Church, professional colleagues, family, and friends. But if he had the impact that I believe he did, was there anyone outside of this circle who could shed light on him? I found my answer with Fathers Obi and Pennington. In the next few paragraphs you will meet them and learn how they are able to give witness to Father Bob.

Celestine Adizue Obi was born in 1938 in the West African Republic of Nigeria. (His birth in Nigeria naturally entitles him to all the rights, duties, and privileges of a Nigerian citizen.) In 1966, Celestine was ordained a priest of the Catholic Archdiocese of Onitsha in Anambra State, Nigeria. During the next 34 years he was engaged actively in the priestly ministry of this archdiocese. In 2000, however, he was sent abroad on a special personal mission to the Catholic Church of the United States of America. The Church in America had prospered during its first 200 years. But after World War II it suffered a rapid shortage of both priests and seminarians. The American Catholic hierarchy sought remedies for this problem everywhere. They even turned to bishops of "third world" nations who had an abundance of priests, suggesting that they send some of their priests temporarily to needy American dioceses. Several thriving dioceses, especially in Africa, responded magnificently to this appeal. Thus, when Bishop Matthew H. Clark of Rochester asked Alberto Obiefuna, Archbishop of Onitsha, whether he might "loan" him an Onitshan priest, the Archbishop sent him one of his ablest men, Father Celestine Obi, S.T.D.

Father Obi spent his first few months in the Rochester diocese in a series of chaplaincies: at the Newman Center of Brockport College (University of the State of New York); and at two Rochester hospitals, Park Ridge and St. Mary's.

Then, from 2001 to 2005, he was resident chaplain at the Motherhouse of the Sisters of Mercy of Rochester and, concurrently, an extern chaplain at Rochester General Hospital. From 2002 to 2005 he lectured at St. Bernard's School of Theology and Ministry, a graduate school conducted by the Diocese of Rochester. Meanwhile he remained available, of course, for various sacramental and educational duties, and for spiritual direction.

Father Celestine and Father Bob first met at one of the monthly "priests' suppers" at Holy Cross Church in Rochester. The pastor of Holy Cross, Father Thomas Wheeland, had for several years been inviting a dozen or so of the local priests to share with him a Sunday evening home-cooked meal. Father Obi and Father Bob both liked this simple morale-building practice. Father Celestine calls the Holy Cross get-togethers an opportunity, particularly helpful in times of stress, to celebrate just being alive and being priests. But it was not until 2002, when Father Bob moved into the Mercy Motherhouse, that he and Chaplain Obi had time to discover their own common interests.

Like Father Bob, Father Obi is a history buff. He perhaps first revealed his own historical bent when he read the revised edition of Father Mac's history, *The Diocese of Rochester in America, 1868 – 1993*. Father Celestine the scholar was attracted to Father Robert the scholar. The African priest found this American priest "cheerful, gracious, approachable, and obviously well-informed." Yet at the same time Father Bob was "selfless and simple." "Don't expect him to pontificate," Obi would caution. "The Prof is still a learner – he's humble, with frankness."

Even the nickname "Prof" that Father Obi gave to Father Mac was a tribute to his exhaustive learning.[5]

When Archbishop Obiefuna loaned Father Obi to Bishop Clark in 2000, he had not yet decided the terminal date of this American mission. Midway in 2005, however, Father Celestine was notified by the archbishop's office that his transatlantic task was now finished and that he should return home. Fly back he did, to resume his part in planning the future of this archdiocese's amazing population of more than 1,440,300 Catholics!

Doctor Obi's many Rochester friends were naturally sad to have him return on September 30, 2005, to his African homeland. They thank him for the assistance he gave not only to the Diocese of Rochester but to the whole Catholic Church in America.

Aware of his close friendship with Father Bob, we co-authors of *A Priest Forever* invited Father Celestine to jot down some reflections on "Prof" to be printed in our biography. Here is a summary of his brief but discerning reply.

---

[5]   Father Bob, reading our manuscript, intervened with a comment: "If we are both somehow entitled to the designation 'scholar,' it is Father Celestine who is the true scholar. Look at his academic status, for example! In Rome he won a Doctorate of Sacred Theology (Pontifical Urban University). In Paris he won an M.A in Catechetics and Pastoral Theology (Institut Catholique de Paris), plus a Ph.D. in Anthropology (Sorbonne). In London he won yet another M.A in Church History (School of Oriental and African Studies, University of London)."

After seriously pondering Father Bob's "dignified priesthood" (his forty-three years of "priest making" within the seminary and, likewise, in the wider world, his constant promotion of Christian culture), Father Celestine could reach only one conclusion: that Father McNamara was called to a very particular mission, the living out of the priestly life in all he did. (This would not necessarily have been a self-conscious motivation: a watchword like "apostolic" might be stimulant enough.) "Unfazed by challenges and with no hankering after glory, he had ripened into a genuine priest in thick and thin... a kind of touchstone for the priests of the Rochester diocese and laity – a touchstone of authenticity in living the Christian life.

"He was a genuine follower of Christ, and Prof *listened* to Christ."

The Second Ecumenical Council of the Vatican (in session 1962-1965) made many changes in the Church's earlier legislation. One of these changes was the acceptance of Catholic participation in the Ecumenical Movement, an international organization formed by non-Catholic Christians to promote a positive dialogue toward Christian unity. After that happy authorization, Roman Catholic seminaries in particular began to establish contacts with the clergy and faithful of the movement's member churches. One of several interchurch episodes at St. Bernard's was the replacement in 1973 of its last Catholic priest-librarian with a young man who was both a schooled librarian and a member of the Episcopal Church.

When the last Catholic priest-librarian retired in 1973, Father Joseph P. Brennan, then rector of St. Bernard's, advertised this library opening in a periodical used by library professionals. Of the several applicants, Jasper Pennington seemed to be the best qualified, so Father Brennan invited him to come to Rochester for a final interview. But an Anglican layman as librarian in a Catholic seminary? No issue: library science is recognized as a technical profession. However, after winning his library diploma, layman Jack had decided to join the Episcopal clergy and was just finishing his theological course at the Episcopal Seminary in Sewanee, Tennessee (although he would not be ordained to his Anglican priesthood until 1974). At this point some Catholics might have wondered whether priestly status would make him still less acceptable as librarian in a Catholic theological school.

29

They *might* have wondered. They *might* also have asked. But nobody *did* ask.

Three cheers for ecumenism!

The success of the appointment depended basically on two things: the character of Deacon Pennington and his skills as a library director. He had a rather fierce red beard, but his inner self was gentle, judicious, and jovial. The seminary faculty took to him readily. Father Brennan asked him from the start to take an active part in all faculty meetings. This was a wise measure; Father Pennington's wit and his divergent views made him a welcome figure at faculty sessions. And when the seminarians returned for the fall semester they, too, judged the new librarian to be "all wool and a yard wide." (A term derived from the garment industry, meaning of high quality and/or genuine, excellent.)

Father Pennington proved no less successful technically as library director. He completely reorganized the books according to the Library of Congress cataloguing system and in other ways updated its functioning. But his major achievement was the foundation of the Bishop Fulton J. Sheen Collection of books and other documents.

Bishop Sheen, the great preacher of the early television age, was 71 when named sixth bishop of Rochester, New York (October 21, 1966). Installed on December 15, 1966, he worked vigorously to communicate the ideals of Vatican II, but he resigned his office early, in October 1969, and was designated Titular Archbishop of Newport (England). He did not leave, however, without donating to St. Bernard's library a large number of volumes from his own library, along with other items from his personal files. Pennington worked closely with Archbishop Sheen in organizing these materials, and Sheen came up from New York to preside at the collection's final dedication on September 27, 1976. Even after the archbishop's death on December 9, 1979, the library director continued to add many valuable items to this rich depository. In 1995 the Archbishop Fulton J. Sheen Collection was permanently housed in the archives of the Diocese of Rochester. Of late, especially given his cause for sainthood, there has been an upsurge of curiosity about Fulton Sheen as a public figure in American secular and religious history. His biographer, Kathleen L. Riley, does well to point out that "the [Sheen] Collection remains an essential starting place for those interested in the life and times of Fulton Sheen."

Jasper Green Pennington was deeply saddened by the necessary closing of St. Bernard's Seminary in 1981. Since day one he had felt at home there. But putting up the shutters at "the Rock" was too hectic to allow due time for credit-giving. That meant specifically that Father Pennington had never been given official praise for his unique contributions to the seminary and to the Diocese of Rochester.

Let Father Joseph P. Brennan speak now, for the record: "We were very fortunate to have Father Pennington on board. He was a first-class associate."

When he left Rochester in 1981, Pennington transferred briefly to the Episcopal Diocese of Maine where he was assigned to a rectorate. In 1983, he rejoined the Episcopal Diocese of Michigan and was appointed rector of the Church of St. Luke in Ypsilanti. He had ample free time, however, to devote to researching and writing Church history and giving a university course in comparative religion. His bishop named him historiographer of the Episcopal Diocese of Michigan (1985 – 2007).

Aware of his close association with Father Bob in historical and archival matters, we invited Father Pennington to write a memoir of his Rochester years. He kindly complied with the following brief but vibrant reminiscences:

1. *His first visit to St. Bernard's, 1973. He meets Father Brennan.*
"With some trepidation I came in faith, and through the efforts of Mrs. M. Jay Byam, the library secretary, Father Bob was dispatched to come for me at the airport. He was not sure why I was there; I was not sure who he was, but we seemed to have a meeting of the minds immediately as he brought me to the faculty lounge after a trip through the somewhat labyrinthine halls of St. Bernard's. And all during this time I was made to feel at home; and one would never have guessed that Bob was probably mystified about what to do with me! 'The Rock' was a rather intimidating place and I began to be a bit anxious about my visit. However, by the time Father Brennan appeared in the lounge, my anxieties vanished and it felt like I had just arrived home.... I have realized that God brought me there [St. Bernard's] to further and deepen my own spiritual life... a kind of finishing school which

few of my classmates had the privilege to enjoy before 'being let loose on the Church,' as one of our bishops was wont to say! And St. Bernard's provided a wonderful family community for my wife Carole and our three children Amy, Thomas, and Sarah, all of whom remember with affection and hilarity their life and experiences with 'The Rock' community…. I look back on those years with great thanksgiving and a deep appreciation for the faculty and students of that place."

2. *Father Jack and Father Bob*

"Throughout those years, Father McNamara was a constant source of companionship as we shared our historical interests and developed the library and archives. As I began to gather the Sheen archives and to talk with the Bishop [Sheen] about his long ministry, Father McNamara was a constant source of encouragement and constructive suggestions. Among the many gifts he brought to me were an interest in the Liturgical Arts Society, the work of Adelaide Bethune and Edward Catich, and the St. Leo Guild. Since Rochester, the drawing by Ade Bethune known as the 'Baptism of Christ' has been made into both an embroidered hanging and a quilted banner, both prominently displayed in Episcopal parish churches.

"Throughout these years, Father McNamara's scholarship in Roman Catholic history in America has inspired my own investigations into the religious history of priests and explorers in the mid-1600s. And so I learned what many generations of seminary students had already learned at St. Bernard's: that Father Bob was a treasure indeed, one of God's marvelous gifts whose light brought growth and growth again. May God keep him always in his love and favor!"

An ecumenical testimony, for sure!

CHAPTER THREE

Growing Toward Grace

In chapter one, we spoke mostly about Father Bob's childhood. In this chapter we shall interview him about his schooling and early life as a priest. What will he reveal to us, for instance, about his curious personal transition from a prospective English literature Ph.D. aspirant to a startled professor of Church history, self-educated as he terms it "in the saddle"?

Utterly charmed by his eight years at St. Mary's School in Corning, he not only responded with ease to the mental and spiritual training he received from the Sisters of Mercy, but he also valued their recognition of his artistic bent, a family trait that would serve him well. One picture he drew, of which he was proud, was of a pirate. This picture has been incorporated, at his request, in this book. It was Father's love of art and his artistic ability that led him to teach courses in art history and to assist in the designing of some of the altars in the diocese.

Let us now ask Father Bob what was going on in his mind when he entered Corning Free Academy (C.F.A.), a public high school, in September 1924.

"Corning has never had a Catholic high school," he said, "and I found it somewhat difficult to adjust to this secular academy. But I imagine that even those in our class of 1928 who were accustomed to a lack of religious reference in the classroom might also have taken a while to appreciate the quality of education at C.F.A." However, looking back at his schooling in 1924-1928, Father Bob remains grateful for the acquaintances it gave him with the non-Catholic American outlook at its best.

Interviewer Ann: "Are you all set, Father, to be questioned?"

Father Bob: "I'm not sure, Ann. Since we began this project, I have been thinking up answers to your questions without knowing what the questions were. Here's what I would be happier doing: I would like just to talk to you first about my life chronologically from 1924 on -- through high school, through colleges, through theology study, and through early priesthood. I would leave my years as a 'public figure' for later on. I doubt I should be brief, I fear; but you would at least get the whole story. Is that workable?"

Ann: "I think it could work, provided you would allow me to interrupt you, when necessary, with questions."

Father Bob: "Of course. Early in my high school career a question arose that involved the secularity of C.F.A. It was a question very Catholic, and very personal. I have told you about my silent acceptance of God's calling me (eventually) to the priesthood. Now, the faculties of Corning Free Academy were properly insistent that high schoolers should be thinking about preparing for a lifetime career. My English teacher, Miss Dorothy Veysey, was competent in advising me to major in English literature. This would qualify me for a career as a teacher-writer. Countless Catholic priests have quietly earned a livelihood as men of letters. But I was not yet ready to announce that my main livelihood would be Holy Orders. C.F.A. advisors were certainly able to direct me in the choice of a literary profession, but they could never have coached me in theology. Therefore, I resolved to postpone announcing my real future – the clerical future – until I had finished high school, college, and graduate school. Thus when people questioned me about my projected occupation, I could truthfully reply 'literary.'

"It was not difficult to confirm my intention with my interest. In C.F.A. I was on the staff of, and wrote much for, our student magazine *The Stator*. At Georgetown I also wrote for the *Georgetown College Journal* and ended up as its editor. In 1931, I even ventured to compete for Georgetown's literary prize, the Lynch-Pendergast Medal. My essay was 'Phases of American Religion in Thornton Wilder and Willa Cather.' I won the medal! Furthermore, I also won its publication in the *Catholic World* (New York). This was my first semi-pro literary effort, decorated and remembered. Aha! I thought; I am now a published author! I was as pleased as punch, although on the vain side I fear.

"I had several motives for going to Harvard in 1932. Georgetown (est. 1789) was still a small, homey institution in the early 1930's. Harvard (est. 1636) was already vast, sedate, and impersonal, but it impressed me nonetheless by its self-confidence, high standards, its many facilities, and its peerless faculty. I tried to enroll in the fabulous Shakespeare course of Professor George Lyman Kittredge, but as usual its seats were oversubscribed; so I settled for his class on Old English (a treat in itself). Professor Fred Norris Robinson's course on Chaucer was a marvel. His classic text, *The Complete Works of Geoffrey Chaucer*, was published while I sat under him, and I well remember his reading Chaucer as Chaucer would have read himself.

"My favorite professor at Harvard, however, was Jeremiah Denis Matthias Ford, Jr. (1873-1958). A native of Cambridge, Massachusetts, Ford was the son of an Irish Catholic immigrant couple; but Jeremiah Sr. and Mary Agnes Collins Ford had the wisdom to encourage Jeremiah's passion for non-English languages. After earlier studies in Ireland and England, he entered Harvard in 1894 and earned a Ph.D. in romance philology (1897). The faculty had already added him to their number in 1895. They held him in high esteem and granted him major advancements until his retirement in 1948. For all the intimacy with the 'Yard,' he became an international teacher, writer, editor, and consultant in American and European academic affairs. In 1937 the University of Notre Dame of Indiana awarded him its Laetare Medal, and in 1945 he was elected a member of the French Academy. If the Ford parents deserve credit for supporting their son's ingenious talent, Harvard still deserves credit for recognizing him as a good teacher.

(I say this proudly as the grandson of another Irish-American immigrant couple.)

"I learned much at Harvard that helped me in my teaching. Still I must say: the professor who was most helpful to me was on the faculty at Georgetown. My literary mentor there was the British poet and popular historian Theodore Maynard (1890-1956). Maynard, a convert to Catholicism in 1913, began his literary career with *The New Witness,* an independent British review founded by Hilaire Belloc (1870-1953), with Gilbert K. Chesterton (1874-1936) as an associate. Belloc and Chesterton became known as the 'Chesterbelloc,' London's most vocal Catholic questioners of twentieth century secularism. Theodore, shaped in their philosophy, first came to the U.S.A. in 1920 as a lecturer and teacher, and at length settled here permanently for the rest of his teaching, lecturing, and writing life. While at Georgetown I was his student. I became his close friend and in a few instances his associate, for example, in the writing of his popular *The Story of American Catholicism.* Looking back, I realize better today how much he influenced my own literary development. A blessed remembrance!

"But, back to Harvard. I was still willing, in September 1932, to spend the legendary six years needed for a Harvard Ph.D. in English literature. As early as November 3, 1932, however (my twenty-first birthday), I decided to focus on a master's degree, which I could achieve in a single year. This would leave me free to enter a seminary (God willing) in the fall of 1933, better equipped to judge how a Harvard doctorate in English would fit into my future as a Catholic seminarian and priest.

"One of my big concerns about making this educational and career change was the impact it would have on my family. So, I wrote to my mother and told her of my change in plans. Needless to say I was concerned how my mother would react to my news.

"My mother responded to my letter immediately and told me, 'I cannot express to you the feelings I experienced when I read it [your letter]. If God has really called my son to serve him I rejoice, but I feel so unworthy of such a blessing. I wish I might talk to you and hear what brought about your decision: I know prayer has always been your guide.'"

Ann: "Father, that was certainly a very powerful blessing your mother gave to you. That should have made you feel good."

Father Bob: "Yes, Ann, it made me feel very good. It also confirmed my belief that I had, in fact, been correct in accepting my earlier call that I was to become a priest. My mother's blessing stayed with me in 1933 when I left for Rome to begin my studies for the priesthood. I wish parents in today's world would be as supportive to their sons and daughters who are discerning a religious vocation as my mother was to me.

"My new classification as a clerical candidate, my ordination to the priesthood in December 1936, my earliest priestly assignments (1937-1938), and most of all my appointment to the (one-person) Department of Church History at St. Bernard's Seminary now demanded much rethinking. By then, an M.A. or even a Ph.D. in English literature would be irrelevant. What I sorely needed was a course in *history*!

"Happily, the rector of St. Bernard's, Monsignor John F. Goggin, proposed a solution: 'If you teach Church history experimentally for a few years,' he said, 'the bishop of Rochester can give you a study leave to enroll for a doctorate in history at a university of your choice. Then you can return to your professorship, diploma in hand.' I accepted the recommendation as the best arrangement, but I was aware, of course, that for the next several years I would be educating myself as well as my students, a flawed procedure at best! 'Learning history in the saddle,' I termed it. Ironically, still I could not bring myself to accept the old proverb 'The self-taught man has a fool for a teacher.' What I most wanted was to learn history thoroughly, not spottily.

"Around this time God sent me a little message through my Corning pastor. Monsignor James Griffen (1856-1949) of my home parish in Corning reminded me that since St. Mary's was incorporated in 1848, the hundredth birthday deserved a real birthday party that year. Could I write its history for publication in 1948? 'If you begin now, you would have over ten years for researching, writing, and printing.' I asked time to think it over. The more I thought the more I concluded that Providence itself was speaking. This would be my first published book and producing it would give me a fine opportunity to learn the publishing process. I said yes, and he said 'thanks.' The exact date I have forgotten but I suppose it was sometime in the summer of 1938. I began my research at once, determined to do my very best.

"Collecting the facts about St. Mary's Parish was a relatively easy job. Learning how to write them up was twice as demanding. For advice on the latter I turned to an essay by Peter Guilday, 'The Writing of Church Histories.'

"Monsignor Peter Guilday (1884-1947), correctly called 'the first professional historian of American Catholicism,' had earned a doctorate in history at the University of Louvain. He joined the faculty of the Catholic University of America, soon focusing on the neglected field of the Church in the United States.

"*A Century of Grace: The History of St. Mary's Roman Catholic Church, Corning, New York, 1848-1948* was published by the parish in 1948. (We put out a small, slightly altered second edition in 1979.) Its 283 pages, abundantly footnoted, spoke for our intention to present a thorough study. I now see its weaknesses, but I was sure of my ground when I accepted the general principle of historian Peter Guilday regarding American Catholic parishes: that they not be viewed with bias as 'foreign intrusions' into a basically non-Catholic settlement but as, from the onset, real if struggling segments of the early American rural villages. Some of the reviewers and analysts praised this approach because it guaranteed a breadth of view. Mr. W. Allen Underhill, the helpful publisher of the *Corning Leader*, called it 'a very valuable and memorable contribution to all phases of Corning life, religious and civic.' And as late as 1993 Mr. Wendell Tripp, the editor of *New York History*, voiced the same conclusion in *Heritage: the Magazine of the New York State Historical Association* (summer issue, p. 29).

"What is more, my home parish was not the only institution that planned a centennial observance in the 1940s. Corning itself was getting ready to celebrate its own hundredth birthday and I could not escape involvement in that event. Several local history buffs, including long-time friends of mine like stationer Castle Cunnings and his wife Maude, Kenneth Erwin, archeologist Ellsworth Cowles, and C.F.A. art teacher Elsie Clute -- all patriotic civilians of many faiths-- agreed that we could help the city best in its centennial plans by founding a serious-minded local historical society. The Corning-Painted Post Historical Society was created on December 3, 1946. Its charter members numbered 110.

"As a known enthusiast about Corning's past, I *had* to join the new organization. Furthermore, I was apparently the only person then engaged in research on a Corning-related theme. I had already become a picturesque figure in the Corning Public Library, poring over the area newspapers from 1840 to 1940 in an effort to relive chronologically Corning's first ten decades. We agreed that I would write a letter to the *Leader* inviting interested parties to meet us on November 19, 1946, in the auditorium of the Corning World War Memorial Library, to discuss the feasibility of setting up a town historical society. Our invitational letter appeared in the *Leader* on October 29, 1946. Some forty persons attended the meeting of November 19 and voted 'full speed ahead.' The organizational meeting took place on the same spot on December 3, 1946, with Miss Mary McCabe, city librarian and CPPHS co-founder, again playing hostess. I was happy to sign up, of course, and able to be of some assistance. At that time, for instance, I was a member of the American Association for State and Local History; so I turned to that organization for assistance in preparing the initial constitution of the CPPHS. When the time came for electing officers, the membership wanted to vote me into the presidency but I gratefully declined. I was no longer a full-time resident of Corning, so I thought it best to have ardent local residents in charge of this very local new enterprise.

"Eventually we made a little compromise. I consented to hold the presidency for twelve months. My successor would then be elected president in the actual centennial year. We made sure that a resident would be chosen as the second president: Mr. Harry A. Erwin, a descendant like Kenneth Erwin of one of Painted Post's pioneer families. My presidential 'year of three jobs' was exhausting but gratifying; and participation in both the parish and the home-town celebrations remains one of my happiest recollections.

"CPPHS incorporated as an independent society with an educational purpose gradually to be spelled out. In 1968 New York State granted it a permanent charter as an educational institution. In March 1975 we 'went professional,' engaging museologist Phyllis Martin (Mrs. Jack H. Martin) to discover in Corning a suitable building and be director of a CPPHS headquarters/ museum. A year later we purchased the 1796 Painted Post Inn at 59 West Pulteney Street. The society itself restored the building's exterior, mapped out its office space, and turned the rest into a little period museum furnished with antiques from the society's own collection. The year 1976 marked the second bicentennial of the Declaration of Independence. All Corning commemorated this national 'birthday of the United States' on July 4, 1976, by dedicating the new headquarters of the CPPHS, re-titled 'The Benjamin Patterson Inn' in memory of a leading local pioneer who was both a Revolutionary War veteran and a former manager of the old Painted Post Inn.

"Did the CPPHS fulfill its primary purpose of assisting the city during its centennial year? Yes, and with dignity, I think. A good number of our members accepted chores to perform. Mine was to write a multi-week column for the *Leader* on Corningites, 'The Good Old Days,' attributed to the pen of 'The Old Chronicler.' But has the society also survived to fulfill its more demanding long-range aim, 'to collect historical data and to diffuse the knowledge of local history'? Yes, it has survived and persevered. This is not the place for a full history of the CPPHS, but as a charter member, I feel it is important to recall at this point not only its beginnings but its rather remarkable achievements.

"The society's main educational function is the instruction given to adults and school children by a team of trained docents. Where else can their instructor better communicate the spirit of a century ago than in a museum full of the tools of 'heretofore'? We must know and appreciate our American ancestors in order to thank them properly.

"The CPPHS had not waited until 1976 to do honor to Ben Patterson, who epitomized the American pioneer. Working with the Painted Post Masons, the local community and the New York State Legislature, they had succeeded in 1959 in attaching his name by law to a New York State bridge at the west end of Corning. The Patterson Bridge Monument was dedicated on April 30, 1959, at an official state ceremony. Governor Nelson A. Rockefeller was on hand to congratulate the local leaders.

"But the guest speaker who attracted special interest was Robert Benjamin Patterson of West Hartford, Connecticut, the great-grandson of our honored pioneer. I was especially happy to have him there. He was one of my former students at St. Bernard's Seminary, although he had left St. Bernard's in 1957 to embrace a long career as a lay historian. Having won a Ph.D. in history, he was engaged by the University of South Carolina in 1962 and would retire from that institution in 1983, by then an internationally recognized specialist in medieval history. Still a graduate student when he spoke at the bridge dedication in 1959, he cited his admirable ancestor as a patriot in war and peace, a champion of the underdog, a sincerely religious man, and a possessor of the other great virtues upon which our country was founded – himself a bridge between America past and America present.

"At our tenth anniversary, CPPHS was fortunate to have New York State historian Dr. Albert B. Corey as our featured speaker. He was amazed at our long life. 'Your society is lucky,' he said, very frankly. 'You have survived for a decade. Groups like yours are constantly creating local history societies that unfortunately are dead before their first birthday.'"

Ann: "Back to Corning."

Father Bob: "Corning had been a humdrum little industrial city in the mid-twentieth century. Tourists had usually bypassed it. In the late 1950s, however, the whole town set about changing all that. Here the preliminary leader was Corning Glass Center, a unique monument to the world's glass working industry. The center comprises a Hall of Science and Industry, where glass products are displayed; the Steuben Glass Factory, where the whole process of blowing and engraving is demonstrated; and the Corning Museum of Glass, a non-profit educational corporation chartered by the Board of Regents of the State of New York, embracing exhibits of glass throughout the ages plus an extensive library of the art of glass manufacture.

"From then on Corning became an international shrine of glassmaking, visited each year by thousands of tourists. The Corning Glass Works (renamed Corning Incorporated in 1989) worked creatively and generously with the whole city to raise it to new levels of updating and self-appreciation. The Corning Glass Center, built by the glass works at the center of town in 1951, summarizes the whole aim: to convert a prosaic factory town into a glass museum and glass library locale.

"This was not tinsel! In December 1951, the Corning Glass Works Foundation was organized to award financial grants for programs designed to benefit the company and its employees. A major achievement of the foundation in Corning was the establishment of yet another glass-related showplace, the Rockwell-Corning Museum.

"Corningite Robert Rockwell, Jr., owner of the city's Rockwell Department Store, had been a dedicated collector of assorted Americana since 1960. He gathered more works of art, children's toys, prints, firearms, paintings by western artists like Frederick Remington, and especially choice items from the art glass works of Corningite designer Frederick Carter. Eventually, Bob Rockwell and his wife Hertha decided that their collection should be placed in permanent display for the public of Corning itself. The city of Corning offered its old City Hall to house the exhibits; Corning Glass Foundation gave a generous donation; and the Rockwell

Museum opened in 1982. Like the Corning Glass Center, the ever-expanding Benjamin Patterson Inn 'village' and all the other improvements of what might be called the Corning Renewal, the foundation had done its best to turn a grimy little town into a tourist mecca. By August 31, 1965, eight million tourists had visited the Corning Glass Center.

"The effective leader in making the city a cultural hub fit for a Fortune 500 company was, of course, the Corning Glass Works. Founder Amory Houghton Sr. (1812-1882) had brought Corning its first glass factory in 1868, as a family owned firm. His descendants who served as president were able bodied men, and they manifested a genuine interest in the social and cultural welfare of the whole Corning area. Most of Corning's twentieth century renaissance took place while Amory Houghton (1899-1981) was president. As an industrialist, educator, federal official, congressman, and diplomat, he particularly exemplified his family's interest in the local community. The motivation of this notable man was clearly related to his pride in being a native of Corning. During the same years his first cousin Arthur A. Houghton had likewise been a stellar benefactor of the Corning area, especially as founder of the Corning Community College.

"One of the most obvious cultural benefits that Corning derived from its renewal was the addition of many new talented citizens. The opening of the museum and library of the center, along with other developments, made it necessary to import into the city a number of specialists and their families. These varied personnel, often highly educated, were an intellectual and cultural asset to the whole locality. Several of the newcomers joined the CPPHS and proved to be able leaders.

"One thinks of such couples as Dr. John (Jack) Martin and Phyliss Martin, and museologist Paul N. Perrott and Joanne S. Perrott.

"Jack Martin was primarily a librarian and professor of English but, as his obituary puts it, 'his intellectual curiosity and scholarly insights were boundless.' In ways too numerous to specify, this sunny man came to be one of Corning's chief teachers,

writers, editors, executives, benefactors, and 'rescuers.' He and
Phyliss Martin were a rare match. As director of the Patterson
Inn complex, she created its operation with a sure hand. Kindred
spirits, they worked together, wrote together, traveled afar together,
and were always really happy to return to their home in Corning.
Jack Martin was also a specialist in Japanese painting who became
director of the library at Corning Community College and was
later affiliated with the Corning Glass Museum.

"Another such was Paul Perrott who worked at the Corning
Glass Museum as an assistant from 1951 to 1961. He became the
director in 1961 and served in that capacity until 1971 when he left
to go to the Smithsonian. Both Martin and Perrott served terms
as presidents of the CPPHS.

"In this shrine to crystal, they are truly GEMS.

"But here I am wasting your time! Have you any specific
questions about my coming of age?"

Ann: "Yes, I have one perplexing question several have asked:
Isn't it odd for a priest to be a historian?"

Father Bob: "That is a puzzler! It makes me wonder whether
the questioner knows what a priest is and what a historian is. As
such the query is unanswerable. But I'll give it a try.

"A priest is one who is ordained to pass on the truths Christ
taught and administer the sacraments Christ initiated. A historian
is one who records both the good deeds and the misdeeds of his
fellow human beings. Whenever, in the discharge of his priestly
duties, any priest is called upon to report an event or advocate a
candidate he must observe historical objectives. But there are also
many priests who can be called eminent professional historians,
like Pope John XXIII who specialized in Italian Church history.
In 1960 I met this great pontiff as one in a long line of pilgrims to
the Vatican palace. Speaking Italian I told him I was a professor
of Church history in Rochester, NY. The Holy Father commented
in Latin: 'Historia testis veritatis!' [History bears witness to the

truth.] A kiss of his ring, a minimal dialogue, and a blessing given and received: all this took only a few seconds of his time; but he handed on to me and other priest historians a fruitful new motto to ponder. Memorable!"

Ann: "The truth, the whole truth, and nothing but the truth!"

Father Bob: "Yes, but remember the historian, or anybody else, can't know the *whole* truth. I must be content with what any person does or says that has been seen or heard. Nobody can know what he is thinking. That would be guessing! A guesser is not a historian; he is more likely a novelist."

Ann: "Thanks for the explanation. That was going to be my second question!"

Father Bob: "Good! And now let me add that regarding objectivity, my determination to take the broad view of truth has pretty much protected me from betraying it. Bishop McQuaid and one of his priests, Father Thomas O'Flaherty, were embattled from 1868 to 1892. Father O'Flaherty, suspended for serious reasons, used the press to misrepresent Bishop McQuaid as a despot who overruled the will of the parishioners. While the bishop could be strict, the suspension of Father O'Flaherty was necessary. Taking a broad view of the incident protected the bishop, priest, and diocese from betrayal."

Ann: "Father Bob, I have a question. One criticism I have heard of you is that when you write about any person or situation you always look for the good. Sometimes it seems you tend to sugar coat things rather than say anything negative. I understand that Bishop Sheen was alleged to have said that Father McNamara's version of history was made up primarily of sugar. I also heard that if a recipe for writing history were to be offered on your behalf it would include certain empathy, upliftedness, and gentleness; that you took care to be charitable in all situations. In your career as a priest, writer/author, and historian you would have been in a position to see many situations that were at best terrible; yet, you always found something nice to say. As a historian shouldn't you have been more open about the negativity?"

Father Bob: "You're right, Ann. I have seen many less than desirable situations in my life. Yet I remember what Jesus said about loving those who do not love you or who you find it hard even to tolerate. 'Love one another' was an example I tried to teach through my writing, and there is nothing that says the truth can't be stated positively. I'm also a person who likes peace and harmony. In the end the final judgment is left up to God. As you know, I prefer to stay non-judgmental, even in my writing. Besides, Ann, a little sugar isn't bad for you!"

Father Bob as an infant with his mother

Father Bob's pirate picture

Feeding birds at Assisi

Father's ordination with his mother

Casa Chapel in Rome, Italy

First Holy Communion

Wedding

Baptism

Father with Bishop Kearney

Father with Bishop Sheen

Book signing with Bishop Clark

Father McNamara-The Legend

CHAPTER FOUR

A Less Typical Calling

In previous chapters we have shown our readers many people who were witnesses to Father Bob's character. We have also shown what prompted him to obtain the education he did and how he continued to educate himself. While the majority of priests go into parish work, Father Bob walked down a different path. In this chapter we shall see that path.

Ann: "Father, in the last chapter you talked about your priesthood, becoming a historian, and looking at things objectively. You also discussed your role in secular activities such as helping to establish the Corning Painted Post Historical Society. Typically, don't most priests go into parish work? In the parish you're dealing with changes and the concerns of your parishioners. I'm hearing you say you didn't do a lot of that, although you were involved in the ecumenical movement, and certainly in your years as a priest you saw many changes in the church and the role of the priest.

"Your focus seems to have been in other areas, such as the historical society, your writing, the history of the Church at large, and in places special to your heart. How would you explain this?"

Father Bob: "Yes, I have had a less typical calling, not as a parish priest but as teacher, historian, and writer/author. My love for writing enticed me to write about my alma mater, the Pontifical North American College (PNAC). I wrote that book because of my love for that college."

Ann: "Is that the book for which you won the award that hangs on your wall?"

Father Bob: "Yes. In fact I will tell you an interesting story about my attending the PNAC. I wrote to Monsignor Griffin at St. Mary's in Corning informing him of my intent to enter the priesthood. He replied and told me he would support my nomination to the priesthood to the Bishop. In his letter he suggested I not say anything about my desire to enter the PNAC. Needless to say, I said nothing about my intent when I applied. But after my studies in Rome I wanted to do something for the college, so I wrote the book."

Ann: "Were you the first to write the history of the college?"

Father Bob: "No, the first was written by Rt. Rev. Henry A. Brann, D.D., L.L.D., and published in 1910. My book was published in 1952, 42 years later, and I'm sure that at some point someone else will build on what I did."

Ann: "Father, did you ever spend any time as a parish priest?"

Father Bob: "For thirty-nine years, while I was teaching at the seminary, I was a 'weekend warrior' at St. Salome's in Irondequoit, where I said one Mass each weekend. After the seminary closed, Monsignor Burns invited me to move to St. Thomas the Apostle where I lived twenty-one years. Another activity I was involved in at Saint Thomas the Apostle was the Legion of Mary. I opened and closed the Adoration Chapel every day. I also wrote Rosary meditations for the Legion of Mary."

Ann: "Father, I understand from some of St. Salome's parishioners such as Sandra and Bill Doran that you gave wonderful homilies, and that many people loved to attend your Mass and hear your homily because they always learned something."

Father Bob: "That was the beauty of it, Ann. I had a relationship with the parishioners without becoming embroiled in parish politics. The parishioners treated me very well. They invited me for breakfast, lunch, and dinner. I'm glad you shared that information about my homilies with me, because a priest never knows how his homilies are received, and it's nice for me to hear that the people appreciated what I said."

Ann: "Was another special interest of yours the theatre? I ask that because two of your brother priests, Fathers Robert C. MacNamara and Sebastian Falcone, told me that one of your duties at St. Bernard's was to direct the Dante Society. I understand this society, which dated back to the beginning of the seminary, was responsible for bringing in famous speakers and putting on dramas and musicals."

Father Bob: "Yes, Ann. I acquired my interest in theatre from my sister Madeline. She had been associated with Corning Summer Theatre for years and had the same sense of humor as I do.

"In my role as moderator of the Dante Society, I produced plays such as *Brother Orchid, The Valiant,* and *The Caine Mutiny.* I also brought in visiting dignitaries such as Charles Brady, Seamus McManus, Father Walsh, and Father Keller.

"In addition I was also able to secure movies for rare moments of student celebration. It was while I was the director of the Dante Society that I also wrote a play, *The Kindly Light.* The play centered on the anniversary of Cardinal Newman's conversion to Catholicism.

"When I moved into St. Thomas the Apostle rectory, Monsignor Burns asked me to write a weekly column for the church bulletin. I began writing 'All God's Children' in 1982. This lasted for three years (one liturgical cycle).

"In 1985, 'All God's Children' became a column about saints titled 'Saints Alive.' Initially these stories were published close to the saints' feast days; however, after about ten years I revised and republished many of the articles, at the same time writing new stories. As Pope John Paul II beatified and canonized new saints, I wrote articles about their lives.

"The most amusing thing to me is that these articles went from a weekly story in the bulletin to vignettes read around the world on the Internet. I've received correspondence from many people around the world, including members of the family of Pier Giorgio Frassati and others who have corrected some of my information.[6]

"In addition, I wrote histories of several parishes in the diocese. These included Sacred Heart Cathedral, Christ the King, St. Thomas the Apostle, and St. Patrick's in Mumford, N.Y. Another piece I wrote for the Corning-Painted Post Historical Society was *Jack Mack or the Shooting of Ellen Callinan: A Forgotten Tragedy*. While one might say this is not within my purview of historical research and writing, it is nonetheless a piece of Corning's history. I also edited several articles."

Ann: "Father Bob, one of your friends, Father Sebastian Falcone, told me you have a great interest in working through the backgrounds of the 'champions of the church.' Did you ever work on a cause that helped beatify or canonize a church champion?"

Father Bob: "Yes, Ann, I did. A cause on which I worked was Blessed Grimoaldo Santamaria. Blessed Grimoaldo had and still has relatives in Rochester. His family had been affiliated with Holy Cross Church, which has a celebration in his honor every year around his feast day November 19."

Ann: "How did you first become involved with Blessed Grimoaldo's cause for canonization?"

Father Bob: "When Blessed Grimoaldo's cause came before the Rochester Tribunal in the 1950s I did not take a part in it, but it caught my attention. I followed the case over the next several years. In January of 1994, Ms. Ida Turan was notified by Father Giovanni

---

[6] Father Bob continued supplying lives of the saints for the St. Thomas bulletin until a few months before he died. See the parish's website: www.kateriirondequoit.org.

Cipriani, the Superior Provincial of the Passionists, that her uncle was going to be beatified. This is the second step in the process of canonizing someone. Based on my work as a historian and with the archives, I became the diocesan person assigned to work on his case.

"As you know, Ann, there are three steps in the process of canonization. The first step is the gathering of evidence that the person is worthy of an investigation into his or her sanctity. In his case, Blessed Grimoaldo's sister and mother had begun a campaign to prove his sanctity, which his mother had documented from his childhood. Although Blessed Grimoaldo never lived in Rochester, his immediate family, including his mother and sister, did. They were the ones who brought his holiness to the attention of the diocese and really promulgated his cause. Between the two of them, they laid the groundwork that would eventually open the cause to his potentially being canonized.

"Once this happens, the next step is beatification. In order for a person to be beatified a miracle must be attributed to the Servant of God, verified after his/her death. The miracle must be proven through appropriate canonical investigation.

"The next step is canonization. In order for a person to be canonized, another miracle is required, again attributed to the intercession of the beatified. When a beatified is credited with a miraculous intervention, it is deemed he or she has direct access to God and thus is able to obtain special graces. A miracle is defined as something that would supersede the laws of nature and for which there is no ordinary cause.

"I'm happy to report that Blessed Grimoaldo was beatified in January 1995. At the first Mass in Rochester for Blessed Grimoaldo, which occurred on September 16, 1995, at Holy Cross Church, Bishop Clark asked me to give the homily. In my homily I said Blessed Grimoaldo was both ordinary and extraordinary. I also said he was given to us by God as a wrong way sign for a society that has gone astray. Blessed Grimoaldo was the antithesis: for the greed our society preaches, Grimoaldo preached poverty; for our society which is obsessed with sex, Grimoaldo preached chastity; and for our society which preaches self-serving and rebellion, Grimoaldo preached obedience. My belief, Ann, is that Blessed Grimoaldo is a saint given to us by God for youth, families, and hope.

"After his beatification I remained involved in his cause for sainthood. I worked with the Turan family to promote Blessed Grimoaldo's cause and I commissioned an icon of him. I gave the icon to Holy Cross Church, where it is today. It is used every year on November 19 for the celebration of his feast day." At his request Father's complete homily from that Mass is included in the appendices.

Ann: "Father Bob, were there other people whom you surmise could be 'champions of the church'?"

Father Bob: "Yes, Ann, there are three more that I can think of quickly: Father Nelson Baker, Blessed Kateri Tekakwitha, and Catherine McAuley. Let me start with Father Baker.

"Father Baker had been a priest stationed at St. Mary's Church in Corning. While he was there he was alleged to have performed three cures. One of these was a woman named Katherine Dwyer (Kate). When she was about 18, she caught typhoid fever. Father Baker blessed her with holy water from Lourdes and she recovered. This was of great interest to me, as later on she married my father and had five children with him. Father Baker was in Corning for about one year before he returned to the Buffalo area where he continued his ministry, which included building a basilica to Our Lady. Today it is known as Our Lady of Victory.

"Blessed Kateri Tekakwitha, a Native American, lived in the Fonda, NY, area before going to Canada. She was orphaned as a small child when a smallpox epidemic killed both of her parents and her younger brother. This epidemic left her face scarred and gave her poor eyesight. Her uncle and aunts took her in to live with them. She was baptized by the Jesuits. Because of her religious beliefs she was continually persecuted by her people. This persecution became so intense that she had to flee to Canada where she joined a village of Indians who had also converted to Christianity. She died in Canada when she was 24.[7]

"Catherine McAuley was born in Ireland in 1778 to a family of some financial means. After her father's death in 1783, her family's savings were lost but she never forgot her Catholic faith which her father had instilled in her. As time went on she became a companion to an elderly wealthy couple who converted to Catholicism before they died. This was in part due to Catherine's teaching and practice of her faith. Upon their death, they left much of their wealth to Catherine, who continued to care for the poor and sick. In time she founded an organization known as the Sisters of Mercy. As you know, Ann, I have a special place in my heart for the Sisters of Mercy. They taught me when I was a youngster at St. Mary's School in Corning and are now caring for me at the McAuley Residence in Rochester.

"These three people went against the norms of society and reached out to help the poor, the sick, the uneducated, and people a lot of us would shun. By doing what they did they lived out the gospel of Jesus, namely Matthew 25:31-45 which says whatsoever you did for the least of my brothers, you did for me. It is my hope and prayer, Ann, that someday all three of these people will be canonized in the Holy Mother Church."

Ann: "So far we have seen the side of you that promotes church champions and preserves Church history. Clearly this falls within your history and writing purview. Did the laity see a side of you separate from what we are seeing?"

Father Bob: "Let me tell you an interesting story, Ann. On November 3, 2005, I reached my 95th birthday, a milestone to anyone. My good friend, Father Robert Bradler, was determined to do something about it, so he planned a huge reception for me at St. Thomas the Apostle Church. In preparation for the reception on Sunday, November 6, Father Bradler placed a piece in his church

---

[7] In December 2011, the Vatican approved the second miracle necessary for Blessed Kateri's canonization. She was formally declared a saint in October 2012.

bulletin asking for people to assist with baking desserts. Fourteen of the finest cooks in the parish responded and helped prepare a delicious spread. Seventy-five written invitations were mailed out and the reception was listed in two church bulletins, St. Thomas the Apostle and St. Salome. For the celebration approximately two hundred twenty-six people, came to wish me all of God's blessings on my birthday. I cannot begin to tell you, Ann, how pleased I was with this celebration. The St. Thomas choir presented me with a lovely tribute. This tribute said in part:

> *Today, we celebrate the special day of November 3rd, 1910, and we reflect on your past, rejoice in your present, and look forward to all that is yet to be…with joyful hearts.*
>
> *You are a dear and holy priest and friend who has touched our lives in more ways than you could ever imagine. You have brought us closer to Jesus through his sacraments and helped us along our journey to faith. As an eloquent writer, you have given us 'All God's Children,' 'Saints Alive,' and most recently 'Good Old Doctor Mac.'*
>
> *Your strong faith, love for God, charity towards others, wisdom, moving words, and kind and gentle way are an inspiration and blessing to all of us. Your life reflects the love of Christ and your love for the Eucharist is reflected in your words that we will now sing.*

"The choir then sang the hymn 'O Sacrum Convivium' for which I had provided an English translation.

"To have so many people from near and far give up their time on a Sunday afternoon to pay me that tribute is a memory I will always cherish. One of the greatest gifts I received was when they told me how much I had been a vessel of Christ's love and love of the Eucharist. To add another cherry on the cake, I thoroughly enjoyed myself and I know others did, too. God is good. I really hope and pray I can live to be 101 years old and ordained a priest for seventy five years."

Father Bob's wish was not to be granted.

CHAPTER FIVE

The Story, the Gift, and the Promise

In the Preface to her book *Keepers of the Story*, Megan McKenna states that all cultures have individuals whose job it is to be keepers of the stories.[8] These story keepers live their lives "dedicated to preserving, to keeping true, to guarding and protecting what is not theirs alone, but what has been given into their care by others. It is a vocation, a calling, a responsibility and a work that defines them in relation to their people and in relation to other groups and their stories. They live on the words but they never make their living from the words. The tales tell *them*. The stories use their flesh, their voices and their minds, to remain alive and to keep the people alive. The keepers are given words, and are held in sway and bondage by the lifelines of hope, suffering, exaltation, births and deaths, resurrections, and vision: by the Story."

My cousin often referred to himself as a "collector of stories." He felt that in that capacity he could preserve pertinent information and historical data for both the Church and society. It was in that vein that he started the archives of the Rochester Diocese and helped found the Corning Painted-Post Historical Society. But his role as a story keeper also allowed Father Bob to reach out to many other people in other ways.

---

8   Megan McKenna, *Keepers of the Story: Oral Tradition in Religion* (New York: Seabury Books, 2004).

In his role as an ordained priest he was able to use the homily at Mass to teach people about both God and man. As we have seen in this book, many people went to his Mass to hear him preach. In his role as a teacher at St. Bernard's Seminary he was able to teach future priests about the correlation between art and Christianity. In his role as a historian he was able to assist Corning in establishing a historical society and preserving and recording its own history. Through his writings he reached out to an audience that eventually became worldwide, his 'Saints Alive' stories on the Irondequoit parish web site being an example. It was through keeping stories that Father Bob understood which legacies needed to be kept and which did not.

So how did Father Bob determine which stories and legacies needed to be kept and which ones did not? Victoria Schmitt, former curator of the history department at the Rochester Museum and Science Center, gave an example of how Father Bob made these decisions.

She was looking for artifacts of ethnic groups in Rochester and she was aware there were various ethnic immigrant Roman Catholic parishes. She knew Father Bob was very knowledgeable of these parishes so she contacted my cousin and requested his assistance. Father Bob then started collecting items from all over for her. One of the items he gave her was his own vestment from Annunciation parish, which had served the Italian community. This vestment had a beautiful filet lace on it. He also obtained for her written histories of a number of parishes. Ms. Schmitt said this was just like my cousin to donate something that he owned and to obtain the histories for her. She also told me that Father Bob was an unsung hero of community service because these objects were not only religious in nature, they reflected different ethnic groups which are an important part of the community. It's interesting to note that, by doing this, Father Bob repeated what he had done with his book *A Century of Grace*. He followed Monsignor Peter Guilday's advice to view Roman Catholic parishes as part of the larger community and not as stand-alone institutions.

When we first undertook our project, there were some things that Father Bob wanted to leave in his legacy and story. One aspect of his legacy was that he wanted people to remember him as a holistic person. He wanted to be remembered not only as a priest, but as a priest who integrated himself into the larger community. There were other ways Father Bob was able to show his holistic approach.

In the foreword Bishop Clark talks about how Father Bob's book *The American College in Rome* showed him the workings of that institution. In his anecdote, Cardinal Dolan states that Father Bob exuded the qualities of a priest that the American College in Rome tried to impart to its students. These views show one aspect of my cousin as holistic.

There were other ways that Father Bob used his writing in a holistic manner. He was able to use his sermons to give simple but effective lessons to help people understand God and the role of Jesus in our lives. He was also non-judgmental in serious situations. In writing an occasional paper for the Centennial of the City of Corning (*Jack Mack or The Shooting of Ellen Callinan: A Forgotten Corning Tragedy*), my cousin was able to show how a murder impacted not only the family but the community. He did it in a manner that was factual but not sensational. In what was his last book, *Good Old Doctor Mac,* Father Bob integrated his personal knowledge of his father with historical and medical information that was pertinent to that time, and wrote a true story of a man near and dear to him. In this book one can see the strong connection between father and son, and yet the son portrayed the father in such a manner as to be honest but not larger than life.

In all he wrote, Father Bob always used his manual typewriter and never learned to use a computer. Whenever the typewriter broke, my cousin didn't stop writing; he simply reverted to using no. 2 pencils and yellow legal tablets. He always worked alone. Changes do occur, however, and this collaborative book was a change for him.

When we started this project, Father Bob and I had an agreement. I would do all the research and writing and he would do the editing. Although neither of us knew it at that time, this really became a gift for both of us. He was able to begin the process of "handing off the baton" to a person who would continue to be a keeper of the story. In handing off the baton, the manner of writing also changed. Now instead of using a typewriter, no. 2 pencils and yellow pads, we were using a computer.

As the method of writing the story changed, so did Father Bob's part in keeping the story. He was no longer the keeper of the story, but the subject. He was able to transition into that role very well. We worked as a team until March 2009.

Toward the end of that month, Father Bob called and asked me to come see him. When I arrived he told me he was not feeling very well and did not know how much longer he could continue to assist me with our project. As we talked we developed a plan to bring the book to fruition. I was fully aware of what this book, his own story in writing, meant to him and I wanted to give him the gift of a finished publication. The plan was that I would take time off on Friday afternoons, come to the Mercy Motherhouse with my laptop computer, and work with him to finish the project. This was the first time we both promised to see our project through to completion. However, God had other plans.

On May 5, 2009, Sister Fran Wegman, director of the independent living center at the Motherhouse where Father Bob lived, called to inform me that Father Bob had been taken to Rochester General Hospital with rectal bleeding. Thus began Father Bob's journey home to God.

That morning in the hospital as I sat with him waiting for test results, Father Bob spoke to me about the book. He told me he wanted to see it completed and he felt he would have enough strength to finish it. Then he did something unusual.

On six to eight separate occasions, my cousin put his hands out as if he were reaching for someone, perhaps for people he had not seen in a long time. He had a smile on his face that was incredible. When I tried to see what he was seeing, all I saw were the walls, the nurse's station, and the people in the hallway. It appeared from his actions that my cousin was seeing something else.

All the time he was hospitalized, Father Bob never forgot about our project. It was so much on his mind that when I walked into his room one night he greeted me with: "Where's chapter three?" When I replied it was home on my computer, he told me to bring it in the next day, along with his no. 2 pencils and yellow tablets. He was so focused on it that he reminded me three times before I left not to forget chapter three.

Although there were some hopeful signs of his recovery, Father Bob returned to his rooms at the Mercy Motherhouse on May 18 with hospice care. Five days later, on May 22, 2009, he entered peacefully into eternal rest.

As we reflect back now on our venture, both my cousin Sue and I hope we have achieved what we set out to do: produce a short biography of a priest whom Bishop Clark called "an extraordinary man." We also hope that this book will encourage all of us to increase our prayers for vocations to the religious life and the priesthood. Our most fervent hope is that Reverend Robert Francis McNamara will always be remembered as *A Priest Forever.*

Appendices

Happy Jubilee, CPPHS!

The Corning-Painted Post Historical Society has reached its 50th birthday. I find that almost incredible! Well do I remember the evening of December 3, 1946, when our wonderful founding group, gathered in the chilly auditorium of Coming's World War Memorial Library, voted itself into corporate existence. Because I was young and pushy, I suppose, the membership elected me president, and we embarked at once on our short-term aim, the promotion of a Corning village centennial observance.

The 1948 celebration went off splendidly. Representing our Society with grace and good humor was my successor in the presidency, Harry A. Erwin, a descendant of one of Corning and Painted Post's pioneer families. But when the parades were over, we had to turn to our more difficult long-term commitment, "to collect historical data and to diffuse the knowledge of local history."

Our earliest projects were a bit amateurish, but they did not lag. Circumstances prevented me from coming to Corning for any but major events. I kept contact with the organization, however, as my fat CPPHS file testifies. To my delight, the society's activities became ever more ambitious and popular, especially after we received our permanent charter in 1968 as a state-approved educational institution.

What contributed most to our permanence, I am convinced, was our "going professional" in March 1975. That year the society engaged a paid director, Phyllis Martin. Her assignment was to provide us with a fitting headquarters and museum of our own. The property purchased in 1976 was theoretically ideal: the 1796 Painted Post Tavern, oldest building in the area. The restoration itself would be anything but easy, however, for the former inn had been badly soddened and mucked by the great "Agnes" Flood of 1972. Nevertheless, within a decade, Mrs. Martin and her team were able to present the community with the Benjamin Patterson Inn, which with its historical out-buildings provides an illustration of "how we were," and serves the society as an archival, educational, and social center.

The relative ease with which this mini-museum was achieved is in large part attributable, I think, to the interested support of the general Coming-Painted Post community. Membership in the CPPHS has grown, but only moderately: from 110 in 1947, to 130 in 1971, to 480 in 1994. We must remember, however, that with the opening of the Corning Glass Center in 1951, Corning became a "museum city." Inevitably, some "museum people" among the citizenry joined the society and gladly shared with it their expertise. One thinks particularly of Paul N. Perrot, Ernestine E. King, Dr. John H. Martin, and Robert and Hertha Rockwell. The list of members also included several persons seriously interested in historical research and writing. Best known among them are Thomas P. Dimitroff and Lois B. Janes, authors of the comprehensive *History of the Corning-Painted Post Area* (Corning, N.Y., 1977, 1991). Naturally, the enthusiastic backing given to the historical society by the likes of these enhanced its prestige throughout the district.

One of our chief fears in the early days of the society was that we might fail to attract younger people into joining our number. Without an upcoming generation to carry on, the organization would be doomed to a short life. Fortunately, the more recent leaders of the CPPHS have laid that fear to rest. The educational programs, the volunteer system, and the stress on family participation all favor a sense of continuity.

Times have changed, of course, over the past five decades. Standards of civility have declined alarmingly in America, even in our smaller communities. Will the old "values" (we used to call them "virtues") be lost irretrievably? A discouraging thought, for although no mention of it was made at the time of its foundation, the Corning-Painted Post Historical Society was conceived of and created on the basis of those very values.

If such values are to be preserved, it seems to me that historical societies like ours can fulfill a positive role, since our very purpose is to remind future generations how much they owe, for what they have and are, to those who "made and preserved us a nation." Could we not, perhaps, strive to impress on youth (and adults as well) the full import of every word in the American Pledge: "I pledge allegiance to the flag of the United States of America and to the republic for which it stands, one nation under God indivisible, with liberty and justice for all." If we could all learn to declare that allegiance with warm conviction, would we not already mark ourselves as people of firm principle?

I congratulate the Corning-Painted Post Historical Society on its golden jubilee, and I pray that its loyal work long continue. I am proud to be one of its members.

(Rev.) Robert F. McNamara
Rochester, New York, 1996

Homily:
Diocesan Celebration
of Blessed Grimoaldo
Santamaria

September 16, 1995

"Having become perfect in a short while, he reached the fullness of a long career" (Wisdom 4:11).

This one sentence from the Book of Wisdom summarizes the whole story of Blessed Grimoaldo of the Purification. Again and again after his death in 1902 at the age of only 19, his devout mother, Cecilia Ruscio-Santamaria, who knew her first born best, predicted to her other children that Ferdinando would one day be beatified. This prediction came true on Sunday, January 29, 1995, when Pope John Paul II bestowed the title Blessed on Grimoaldo Ferdinando Santamaria. Today, Saturday, September 16, 1995, we gather joyfully for the first formal celebration in the Diocese of Rochester of this holy Passionist seminarian.

But why should Rochesterians hasten to honor an obscure native of Pontecorvo, Italy? Because after his death, his younger sister Vincenzina (Jenny) and her husband Frank Panella, and later on his mother Cecilia herself, left Italy for America and became permanent residents of Rochester, New York. All three lie at rest today in Holy Sepulchre Cemetery, and dear Mama Cecilia was buried in 1934 from this very Church of the Holy Cross.

Two of Vincenzina's daughters and a number of her descendants are with us today, and many others long devoted to the Passionist Brother Grimoaldo. We are honored, too, by the presence of a group of distinguished Passionist priests. All three groups pray for his canonization, for they know well the story of his life. But I am sure they will not mind if I tell the rest of you a little about Brother Grimoaldo's career and his virtues.

Why, you may wonder, should the Pope have beatified this teen-ager? I think it was because he found him at the same time ordinary and extraordinary. Grimoaldo was certainly ordinary. He came from an ordinary Christian family. He was a student of only ordinary ability. His sole aspiration was the seemingly ordinary one of serving God and neighbor. But, what was going on inside this youngster's head and heart was anything but ordinary. When he was about six years old, God began to impress upon his mind the greatness of the two commandments: To love God with all one's strength, and one's neighbor as oneself (Mark 12:30-31). Obedience to these commands, Ferdinando came to see with conviction, was the key to heaven. This was what Jesus compared in his parable to a rich treasure unearthed in the field. This was what Jesus called the "pearl of great price" (Luke 10:42). From that revealing moment onward, said his mother, her son held all else in life unimportant. "See how the water flows," he observed one day to his father as they stood on the banks of the river Liri, "so pass the days of our life on earth." He therefore, lost no time in becoming a prodigy of prayer, penance, and tender piety. In 1899, aged 15, with the blessing of an appreciative mother and more reluctant father, he left home to join the Passionist Order, taking the religious name Grimoaldo della Purificazione. His new Passionist family marveled at his effort to obey their holy rule flawlessly, yet with great good cheer. Never was he closer to God than during the terrible eighteen days of illness that ended with his death on November 18, 1902. By then all who knew Ferdinando Santamaria knew that, however ordinary he might have seemed at first glance, he was indeed an extraordinary servant of God, helped by Our Lady to become "Perfect in Christ" (Col. 1:28).

Santamaria had assured his family that he would pray for them in heaven, as well as on earth. They turned to him now for family favors. His fellow Passionists did the same. But only after 1950 did the Italian Passionists decide to acquaint the broader world with their humble confrere.

They also asked his sister Vincenzina Panella to promote devotion to him in the United States.

Now, although she herself had prayed to her brother, Jenny Panella (as she was called in Rochester) was surprised to be asked to share that devotion with those outside the family. Nevertheless, she consented. Under the careful direction of the Italian Passionists, she set up a little shrine in her home. She would tell those who gathered to say a few simple prayers her own recollections of Ferdinando, and the cherished reminiscences of her late mother. Soon a growing number of people from Rochester, Utica, and Buffalo joined her prayer group, and she was able to communicate to her Passionist guides a score of favors attributed to Grimoaldo's intercession. In 1957, when the Vatican asked the then bishop of Rochester, James E. Kearney, to officially interview three Rochester women who had known young Grimoaldo, Mrs. Panella was naturally a key witness. It was she, therefore, who introduced devotion to him into the United States. We are happy to have with us today some of the priests associated with Bishop Kearney's commission of inquiry in 1957-1958. They made a most important contribution to Grimoaldo's beatification.

Finally, what sort of saint is Blessed Grimoaldo, and why has God given him to our day and age?

Time alone will give a fuller answer. Let me tell you my own reflections. What sort of saint is he? Saints, like stars, differ in prominence. God has made them so. I consider Grimoaldo not a big saint, but a little saint, a humble saint -- like St. Therese, the Little Flower, unknown while on earth, but showering roses from heaven -- a saint for every family in the world, in which he becomes the wise elder brother. A generous teen-aged saint ready to help any neighbor in the block.

And, why has God given him to us in 1995? I think he has set up the young Passionist as a wrong way sign for a society that has gone astray. Our generation is greedy; Grimoaldo vowed poverty. Our generation is obsessed with sex; Grimoaldo vowed chastity. Our generation is self-serving and rebellious; Grimoaldo vowed obedience. Our generation, terribly misled by Satan, has declared war on children, not only on the born and the unborn, but on childhood itself; Grimoaldo, however, while manly in frame, in judgment, and in strength, never lost that childlike candor required for the kingdom of heaven (Matthew 18:3). He embodied, as St. Paul puts it, "whatever is honorable, whatever is just, whatever is pure, whatever is lovely, whatever is gracious" (Phil. 4:8). In other words, whatever is wholesome and beautiful in Christian youth. Exactly what the world needs today!

Cardinal Newman, so dear to the Passionists, suggests another perspective on the new Blessed. The Cardinal himself used to pray, "Help me, Lord, to spread your fragrance wherever I go; let me preach without preaching, not by words, but by example." What Newman prayed for, God gave as a gift to Ferdinando Santamaria. Today, says Pope John Paul II, our world has chosen a culture of death, and the stench of its violence has polluted the very air we breathe. But see, Grimoaldo now comes to us, a saint for youth, a saint for families, a saint for hope, ready to help us, like a strong sweet wind, to scatter the toxic smog of sin.

Let us salute him, then, young and old alike, by making our own the first prayer of today's Mass:

> *O God, you constantly present to your Church new models of Christian life. Help us to imitate the tender devotion to Mary Immaculate and the selfless love of neighbor of Blessed Grimoaldo of the Purification, so that we, too, may be the fragrance of Christ on earth and inherit the eternal rewards of heaven. We ask this through Christ our Lord. Amen.*

Robert F. McNamara

Father Bob's Rosary Meditations

THE FIRST JOYFUL MYSTERY:
THE ANNUNCIATION

We begin the fifteen decades of Our Lady's Rosary with the first of the five joyful mysteries: the announcement made by the Angel to Mary of Nazareth.

Before we begin to ponder this happy event, however, we must recall that while the Rosary is addressed through Our Lady, its mysteries -- joyful, sorrowful and glorious -- concern Our Lord primarily and Mary secondarily.

When, therefore, we commemorate the Annunciation, it is the Lord's annunciation. When we meditate the Visitation, it is the visitation to Elizabeth of the unborn Jesus. The mystery of the Nativity recalls his birth to the Blessed Virgin. The mystery of the Presentation recalls his presentation at the Temple by Mary and Joseph. And the mystery of the Finding in the Temple memorializes his rediscovery by his parents, as he first declares his independence of them so that he can undertake the commission of his heavenly Father.

To make this point is by no means to detract from the Mother of God. It is to emphasize her unique role in the Redemption. The Father had chosen her for this singular task. He had, as she would say, "looked upon his servant in her lowliness." Through her the Messiah, the "Light from Light," the "Daybreak from on high," would dwell among us. She would only reflect his glory, mirroring his justice as the moon mirrors the glory of the sun. A subordinate role, yes, but one with which she was well content, and remains well content.

The first joyful mystery is therefore called in the Missal the "Annunciation of the Lord."   We know the story well. St. Luke relates it, quite likely on the basis of Mary's own account, learned from her directly or indirectly (1:26-38). The Archangel Gabriel was sent to Mary, a virgin already engaged to Joseph: a carpenter, yet a descendant of David the King. Gabriel greeted the young woman with startling words, "Hail, favored one [or 'full of grace'], the Lord is with you." When she seemed troubled, he continued, "Do not be afraid, Mary, for you have found favor with God. Behold, you will conceive in your womb and bear a son, and you shall name him Jesus. He will be great and will be called Son of the Most High, and the Lord God will give him the throne of David his father, and he will rule over the house of Jacob forever and of his kingdom there will be no end."

As a vowed virgin, Mary naturally raised the question, "How can this be, since I have no relations with a man?" Gabriel reassured her, "The Holy Spirit will come upon you, and the power of the Most High will overshadow you. Therefore the child to be born will be called holy, the Son of God." As a sign of guarantee the Archangel revealed that Mary's cousin Elizabeth, although now aged and hitherto barren, had likewise conceived a son due for birth in three months, for "nothing is impossible for God."

Mary was thus faced with a more momentous choice than had ever been asked, or ever would be asked, of any woman. As a devout young Jew she knew, at least in general, what the invitation implied. Artists depicting this event show her with a book, the Old Testament containing the prophecies of the Savior-to-come. It was her heel that would crush the head of Satan (Gen. 3:15). It was she of whom the Lord had foretold, "the virgin shall be with child, and bear a son, and shall name him Emmanuel" (Is. 7:14). It was she through whom mankind would be redeemed: IF-IF-IF she would only consent to God's plan. Think of it: the reconciliation of God and man, estranged so long ago through the sin of Adam, was made to depend on the YES of this teen-ager of Nazareth. What a favor to ask! What a commitment to propose!

The great St. Bernard of Clairvaux once gave a moving sermon on the Annunciation and what it implied. In this sermon the saint pretends to be watching Mary anxiously as she ponders her reply. "The angel awaits an answer," he urges her, "it is time for him to return to the God who sent him. . . . The price of our salvation is offered to you. We shall be set free at once if you consent."

Bernard presses her still further, "Tearful Adam with his sorrowing family begs this of you, O loving Virgin, in their exile from Paradise. Abraham begs it, David begs it. All the other holy patriarchs ask it of you as they dwell in the country of the shadow of death. On your word depends . . . salvation . . . for the whole of your race.

"Answer quickly," he pleads. "Speak your own word, conceive the divine Word . . . Why do you delay; why are you afraid? . . . See, the desired of all nations is at your door, knocking to enter. Arise, hasten, open!"

After a moment that seems an eternity, Mary speaks. "Behold, I am the handmaid of the Lord. May it be done to me according to your word."

She had said YES.

At that moment the Word became flesh!

THE SECOND JOYFUL MYSTERY:
THE VISITATION

When the angel announced to Mary that she was to become the human mother of the Son of God, she consented, in all humility. Therefore it is appropriate that in the shrine-church erected over the traditional site of Our Lady's Nazareth dwelling a brass inscription in the floor of the sanctuary should proclaim: "Here was the Word made flesh."

What did the young virgin do immediately after conceiving the Christ child? St. Luke tells us that almost at once she went to visit her cousin Elizabeth, of whose pregnancy with St. John the Baptist the Archangel Gabriel had told her. She "set out," St. Luke informs us, "and traveled to the hill country in haste to a town of Judah." Just what town? Nobody knows for sure. Some think it was at Ain Karim, about an hour west of Jerusalem. Others think it was at Hebron, some 25 miles south of Jerusalem, where the altitude is 1400 feet. In either case it was a long distance from Nazareth -- between 70 and 100 miles. For safety, Mary most likely traveled in the company of others. But Joseph was not with her. Apparently he had not yet been informed from heaven of the pregnancy of his fiancé.

Why did Our Lady <u>hasten</u> to see Elizabeth? Quite likely for more than one reason. Out of charity, for instance, she probably wanted to congratulate her kinswoman personally, and perhaps be of some service to her.

Her main motive, however, was surely more profound. Elizabeth had Zachary and the neighbors to assist her; and, as a matter of fact, Our Lady did not remain with her until John was born. In the Visitation I see, rather, a second, inspired step in the history of our redemption. Mary went to Elizabeth primarily, I think, because God wanted to bring the unborn Jesus into the presence of the unborn John the Baptist, who three decades later would introduce him to the world.

Notice what St. Luke tells us of the meeting of the two mothers-to-be.

Mary had learned from Gabriel of John's conception. Elizabeth knew nothing about the conception of Christ; but as soon as she heard her cousin's greeting, God revealed this to her. "Filled with the Holy Spirit, she (Elizabeth) felt the infant leap in her womb," and she greeted Mary ecstatically: "Most blessed are you among women and blessed is the fruit of your womb!" With the most heartfelt humility, the old woman bowed before her young relative: "And how does this happen to me, that the mother of my Lord should come to me?" The mother of my <u>Lord</u>: Mary did not need to tell Zachary's wife the good news. God had disclosed to Elizabeth in the twinkling of an eye that Mary was the mother of God's Son, for in Hebrew the word that Elizabeth used – *Lord* -- means *God*.

And what of John the Baptist, still growing close to his mother's heart? At the sound of Mary's sweet voice, he leaped in the womb. Was this just a case of the quickening of the five-month-old unborn, kicking vigorously in his maternal nest? It was more than that, I think. It was the fulfillment of Gabriel's prophecy about John to Zachary: "He will be filled with the Holy Spirit even from his mother's womb" (Lk 1:15).

Centuries before the happy meeting of Mary and Elizabeth, Jesus' royal ancestor King David had organized a solemn procession to bear to Jerusalem the Ark of the Covenant. The Ark was that ornate chest made at God's bidding to house the stone tablets on which the Ten Commandments were inscribed. Since Sinai this Ark had remained the symbol and the very locus of God's presence among his chosen people. Along the route of procession, David danced before this sacred chest, a dance of joyful worship and devotion. Now, in the home of Elizabeth and Zachary, John the unborn danced an invisible dance of joy before Christ the unborn, whose presence within Mary made her the true Ark of the Covenant of which Moses' Ark was only a foreshadowing.

Thirty years later, this same St. John, the great Forerunner of Jesus, would meet Jesus face to face. Although he had most likely never set eyes on Jesus, he would now, inspired by God, point him out to his own disciples in the desert, "Behold the Lamb of God. Behold him who takes away the sins of the world." From that day on, John the Baptizer, guided ever by the Holy Spirit, would make straight the pathway of the Savior. But this was not a task newly assigned. The Spirit of God had entrusted him with the role of forerunner three decades before, when Mary visited her kinswoman Elizabeth, and the Spirit bonded together the Son of God and the son of Zachary to launch the redemption of the human race.

THE THIRD JOYFUL MYSTERY:
THE BIRTH OF OUR LORD

In our day Christmas has become far too commercialized, and far too de-Christianized. Even the lovely Christmas hymns and carols, in spite of their artless tunes, can be over-broadcast. They become boring rather than inspiring when they are blasted into our ears from November on. Of course, we <u>can</u> discipline our ears. (I myself refuse to heed any Christmas songs before Christmas Eve.) If we do, we can still find the Nativity a spiritual event: a charming, enchanting, moving feast, which more than any other religious festival brings everybody closer together, at least for 24 hours. Indeed, it tends to unite all creation as man and beast gather to worship a tiny child. This child is the epitome of loving kindness. He represents not only all that is gentlest in human life, but the compelling love God himself has for us, his ungentle, contrary children.

The tender account of the birth of Christ given in the Scriptures has inspired many devout Christians over the centuries to invent further tales about the infancy of Our Lord. These are fiction, of course, but we accept their fantasy as loving improvisations on a true theme. Many of these purport to tell how the animals reacted to the Nativity.

Irish poet Denis A. McCarthy sums it up in his poem "Christmas Legends:"

> Christmas morn, the legends say,
> Even the cattle kneel to pray,
> Even the beasts of wood and field
> Homage to Christ the Savior yield,
> Horse and cow and woolly sheep
> Wake themselves from their heavy sleep,
> Bending heads and knees to Him
> Who came to earth in a stable dim.
> Far away in the forest dark
> Creatures timidly wake and hark,
> Feathered bird and furry beast
> Turn their eyes to the mystic east.
> Loud at the dawning, chanticleer

Sounds his note, the rest of the year;
But Christmas Eve the whole night long
Honoring Christ he sings his song. . . .
And shall we, for whom He came,
Be by cattle put to shame?
Shall we not do so much at least
As the patient ox or the forest beast?
Christmas morn, oh, let us sing
Honor and praise to Christ the King,
Sheltered first in a lowly shed,
And cradled where the cattle fed.

Officially, the birth of Christ was private, unpublicized. But you will notice that God saw to it that the witnesses of the event represented all breathing creation. Mary and Joseph and the shepherds were stand-ins for the Jews. The Three Wise Men were stand-ins for the Gentiles. Even the animals had their deputies: if not the worldwide creatures of legend, at least Joseph's donkey, the stableman's ox, and the sheep of the shepherds.

Why did Jew and Gentile and lesser creatures seem so at peace with God and with each other during these visits? Was it not because they sensed, somehow, that this little Second Adam would give mankind a fresh start?

God the Father, through God the Son, had originally created the universe to operate in an orderly way. He had made the First Adam and the First Eve, and placed them in the first Paradise to rule the earth in peace. He gave them authority over not only man but every living creature; and the animals, at least, showed themselves accepting of his command.

Unfortunately, Adam and Eve fell into sin and were cast out of Eden. The sin of the first parents not only estranged them and their descendants from God, but even from the lesser animals. Apart, perhaps, from our domestic animals, they have never fully trusted mankind since that day of bitter alienation.

Finally, however, God the Father sent his creator Son, the Word, to become man in order to rescue man. This Jesus would do through his redeeming death, meriting for those human beings who accepted him a renewed friendship with the Father. On the final Day of the Lord, Jesus, the Second Adam, would return to earth, judge all men, and assign the worthy faithful, body and soul, to the glories of heaven.

When the world as we know it is renewed under the eternal smile of God, will the animals he created also be there? Turtles and tuna fish, cats and canaries, dogs and dinosaurs? We do not know. They have no immortal souls; yet, as the prophet David says, "All ... beasts, wild and tame, bless the Lord, praise and exalt him forever" (Dan. 3:81). Could God not re-create them all if he deemed it appropriate to have them on the streets and in the fields around the New Jerusalem? Recall that he foretold through the prophet Isaiah a final peaceable kingdom where "the calf and the young lion shall browse together, with a little child to guide them" (Is 11:6). And had Jesus not commanded the disciples to "proclaim the gospel to <u>every creature</u>?" (Mk 16:15)

Whenever this beautiful but wayward earth seems too much to bear, let us always return in spirit to the utter simplicity of the stable at Bethlehem, where the little Second Adam rules in peace over man and animal. Reassured in hope by this Christmas vision, we can say with St. Paul: "The grace of God has appeared, offering salvation to all men. It trains us to reject godless ways and worldly desires, and live temperately, justly and devoutly in this age as we await our blessed hope -- the appearance of the glory of the great God, our Savior Jesus Christ" (Ti 2:11-13).

THE FOURTH JOYFUL MYSTERY:
THE PRESENTATION IN THE TEMPLE

In addition to the moral laws inscribed by God on the twin tablets of stone -- the Decalogue or Ten Commandments -- Moses also prescribed for the Israelites many rules of worship. One ritual law required that a mother come to the Temple in Jerusalem forty days after the birth of her son to make two offerings: one for her own legal "purification," the other to be burnt as a sacrifice of thanksgiving. The offering for purification was a pigeon or a turtledove. The thanks-offering for sacrifice was normally a yearling lamb. But if the mother was poor, she could offer instead two turtledoves or two pigeons, one for purification and one to be burnt as a holocaust in place of the lamb (Lv 12:2-8).

St. Luke tells us how Mary and Joseph complied with these regulations. Devout Jews that they were, they more than fulfilled the requirements. Thus another law commanded that parents present every firstborn child as a special gift to God. This could have been done at the synagogue of Nazareth, but they chose to go to the Temple in Jerusalem to consecrate their son (Ex 13:2, 13), and to "redeem" him with the prescribed alms, due to the priests, of five shekels (Num 3:47, 48; 18:15, 16). Since the birth of Christ had been miraculous, the Virgin Mary had no need to give the sin offering, yet she did so to express her solidarity with the human race. Since she and Joseph were poor, however, they gave the Temple authorities the two doves, the one dove for purification and the other for sacrifice.

What the mystery of the Presentation teaches us, then, first-off, is the lesson of generous obedience to God's law. Not all the laws of the Old Testament were of major importance; yet Mary and Joseph observed them beyond the letter of the law. How often our obedience is calculating, stingy. ("You ask for just so much, Lord, and I give you that, no more.") Shouldn't our obedience rather be lavish, governed not by the norms of haggling but by the norm of love? Love was the motive that prompted the Son of God to become man and suffer for us. Remember, he could have redeemed us by shedding one drop of blood, even the blood of his circumcision. But no, he offered his blood abundantly, to the last drop that flowed from his pierced heart. We, too, should be spendthrift in giving ourselves to God and his laws. Our prayer for the spirit of generosity should be that of St. Ignatius of Loyola: "Receive, O Lord, all my liberty. Take my memory, my understanding, and my entire will. Whatsoever I have or hold, you have given me; I give it all back to you and commit it wholly to be governed by your will. Give me your love and your grace, and I am rich enough and ask for nothing more."

The scenario of the Presentation introduces us to two other admirable people: Simeon and Anna the prophetess. Both were old, wise, and close to God. For years Simeon had been dreaming of and praying for the coming of the promised Messiah. When he saw Jesus, the Holy Spirit inspired him with the realization that this infant was to be the Christ of prophecy. A wonderful reward for his constant prayer, and he knew it. Taking the child in his arms, he uttered thanks to God: Now, Lord, you can call me to yourself, for my eyes have looked upon your salvation. But he warned Mary, as the Spirit instructed him, that her child would suffer contradiction, and she herself great pain.

Then Anna appeared to the little group. She did not speak, but being a prophetess, she also knew that her long prayer-vigils in the Temple had won her the favor of looking upon the Savior. Surely she, too, cuddled him in her arms, although St. Luke does not give us this sweet detail.

Why did God grant such a privilege to this aged couple? Because they had long since learned that the only important aim in life is to be in God's presence. As the psalmist says, "Of you my heart speaks; you my glance seeks. Your presence Lord, I seek" (Ps 27:7, 8). And if heaven was not yet theirs, they sought God in the next-best place, his holy Temple. "How lovely is your dwelling place, O Lord of hosts," the psalmist sings. "I had rather one day in your courts than a thousand elsewhere. I had rather lie at the threshold of the house of my God than dwell in the tents of the wicked. Even the sparrow finds a home, and the swallow a nest in which she puts her young -- your altars, O Lord of hosts, my king and my God" (Ps 84).

We, too, do not share the ultimate consolation of Israel that Simeon and Anna patiently sought: to look on God face to face in heaven. Yet our privilege is even greater than the momentary privilege granted to them at the Presentation. We have Christ with us, day in and day out, in the Blessed Sacrament. I look upon all the faithful – men, women, and children -- who adore Christ in the Eucharist as the Simeons and Annas of today. We may not have achieved the holiness of Simeon and Anna, but we appreciate with them that the closest place to heaven on earth is the House of God. Pondering the Presentation in the Temple, we exclaim, "Happy they who dwell in your house! The Lord withholds no good thing from those who walk in sincerity" (Ps 84).

THE FIFTH JOYFUL MYSTERY:
THE FINDING IN THE TEMPLE

There is a point in the life of all parents, I am sure, when they suddenly realize vividly that their child is neither a part nor a possession of its father or its mother, but someone totally other. They have collaborated with God in bringing this new life into the world, and they have fulfilled their implicit duty to nourish and train him or her in body and soul. Yet the child remains a separate person, body and soul, with a separate mind and a separate free will, bound to work out a separate salvation. How profound is personhood!

While parents are doubtless most aware of a child's individuality when the time arrives for him to "leave the nest," they have probably experienced it off-and-on for years. Even a small child can cause them to reflect when he asks questions that are puzzling or perhaps even profound. I remember a story told by Garrison Keillor, the radio editorialist. He said that his little daughter had once asked him, "Daddy, why did God create Lake Erie?" For that question he simply had no answer. Nor do other Daddies and Mommies have answers for some of the queries of these blessed children of God. God alone knows what is going on in their innocent minds.

If ordinary parents find their offspring mysteriously other, how did Mary and Joseph feel about the growing Jesus? Of course, Jesus was the blood-son of Mary alone, and only the legal son of Joseph. Yet both of them had undertaken the usual parental duties. They would nurture him; coach him, by word and example, in bodily self-care; train him in physical skills (like carpentry); and introduce him to the human processes of reading and reasoning. They would teach him how to get along with other human beings. Most of all, they would raise him in the careful knowledge of the law of God, and its faithful practice.

St. Luke's gospel is the only one to record Mary and Joseph's loss and finding of Jesus in Jerusalem when he was 12 years old (2:41-52). We know the episode well. Joseph and Our Lady took the boy to Jerusalem for the celebration of the Jewish feast of the Passover. He was not with them when their party set out on the return trip to Nazareth, but they figured he was elsewhere in the crowd of friends and relatives who were homeward bound. When they finally learned that he was nowhere among the Nazarean pilgrims, they hurried back to Jerusalem. For three days they scoured the city anxiously in search of him. Finally they discovered him in the Temple intently discussing religious truths with a cluster of rabbis. Apparently the rabbis had gathered to take part in the discussion because they were amazed at the knowledge and wisdom displayed by this youngster.

Reading between the lines of St. Luke, we gather two important points about the training that Mary and Joseph had given to the child Jesus. First, they had seen to it that at Nazareth he was given the best available religious instruction and raised in the most faithful religious observance. Had not his knowledge amazed the rabbis? Was not a Passover pilgrimage to Jerusalem the yearly practice of the Holy Family?

Second, his parents had striven to develop in Christ a sense of responsibility. By the time he was 12, they were ready to allow him some freedom of movement among relatives and fellow townsmen. Were he 13 today, his local synagogue would admit him to the Bar Mitzvah ceremony, an official recognition of arrival at adulthood. Nevertheless, the disappearance of the boy deeply shocked his mother and foster father. Were they tempted for a moment to think that he was showing himself inconsiderate in spite of their years of careful training? We can be sure that Mary, at least, would have suspended any such judgment. But they were puzzled, nonetheless, by his unannounced leave-taking. They were puzzled still more when, on being found, he asked them, "Why were you looking for me? Did you not know that I must be in my Father's house?" The question can be read either "in my Father's house" (the Temple), or "about my Father's business." In either case, he was referring not to his foster father Joseph but to his Father in heaven.

If not at once, still eventually, Our Lady and her spouse came to see in this event an indication not of Jesus' irresponsibility towards them but of his responsibility to God the Father. If ordinary parents have to accept at one point a "declaration of independence" by the children they have raised, the parents of Jesus had to accept the forthgoing of their Son upon the sublimest of all missions. That mission of redeeming all men required that he detach himself to a certain extent from all of them. Some eighteen years after being found in the Temple, he would say: "Who is my mother? ... Whoever does the will of my heavenly Father is my brother and sister and mother" (Mt 12:48, 50). He spoke thus not to disown his own family but to emphasize his role as member and ruler of all families.

Jesus did not disappoint his parents. Unfortunately, today many children disappoint even the most conscientious parents. I heard recently of a family of four raised in the faith by good Catholic parents, none of whom is today a practicing Catholic. When we pray this mystery of the Rosary, let us remember those children who have forgotten or unlearned the lesson of Christian life. If, in answer to our prayers, they die Christian deaths, the Finding in the Temple will be for them, as it finally was for Mary and Joseph, a joyful mystery.

THE FIRST SORROWFUL MYSTERY:
THE AGONY IN THE GARDEN

Agony in a garden? The title of this mystery seems self-contradictory. We think of a garden as a place of peace and beauty. How could it ever become a place of anguish, of all but mortal agony?

Well, however soothing a garden of flowers and shrubs can be when carefully tended, it can lose its charm if neglected; and in winter, of course, it becomes withered and repulsive.

The Garden of Gethsemane was probably well kept all year round, for it was an orchard of olive-producing trees. The fact that Jesus often sought it out as a spot for quiet prayer is proof of its silent charm. But when anxiety troubles the human heart it can rob a garden of the charms that its beauty might normally provide.

When Our Lord visited Gethsemane right after the Last Supper, all the weight of the world's sin was upon him, for he knew that his passion and death were about to begin. That night the garden offered him no peace of mind. Nor were his apostles in any way consoling. James and John and even Peter, the "rock" on whom he would build his church, slept as he prayed. Neither earthly beauty nor the presence of his dearest friends availed him that night. He was to suffer totally alone.

The term "agony" is well applied to that tortured period of prayer. "Agony" comes from a Greek word applied to athletic contests, especially wrestling. In this wrestling match the contestants were Christ the divine and Christ the human. As the Son of God, Jesus knew that he was committed to saving mankind by dying in his human nature. As the Son of Mary, he had all the fears that we have in the face of mental and physical pain; indeed, he had more than the normal fears, since as God he knew exactly what torments to expect. No wonder, then, he said, "My soul is sorrowful even unto death" (Mt 26:38). Wrestlers sweat much in their contests. In Jesus' case, his inner struggle caused him to sweat blood, as St. Luke tells us (Lk 22:44). This was no miracle, but a physical phenomenon, which physiologists call "diapedesis." It is psychosomatic; mental stress can cause blood vessels to rupture. But it can still be considered the beginning of his bloody passion.

Which of us, face to face with a painful trial, a projected operation, for example, does not hope to the last that it can be avoided? Which of us does not even pray for a miracle? Our Lord now prayed in his human mind and will that he might be dispensed from drinking this chalice of suffering. How much he showed himself united to us in our human nature by that prayer! Yet in his divine mind he knew he could not escape death. So, although he prayed to his Father to be spared his sacrifice, he left the decision up to the Father; "Not my will but yours be done." God the Father did not change his own will. The only pity he had on Jesus was to send him an angel to comfort him briefly in his loneliness. (God gives us special strength, too, when we accept a measure of pain according to his holy will.) Let us say, then, that in the great forthcoming sacrifice of Mount Calvary, Christ's human acceptance of the divine will was the grand offertory.

What does this mystery of the Rosary teach us?

First, that Our Lord is not only fully divine but fully human, and can therefore appreciate our own human griefs. As the Letter to the Hebrews puts it, "We do not have in Christ a high priest who is unable to sympathize with our weaknesses, but who has similarly been tested in every way, yet without sin" (5:15). Indeed, whatever human anguish we may suffer, he has suffered far more.

Second, when we pray to God we should not give up quickly if our request is not granted. Jesus prayed in the Garden not once but three times. The more intense his agony, the more intense his prayer.

Third, while we pray for what we think we need, we must leave the decision to grant it in the hands of our heavenly Father: "Not my will but yours be done." Nobody, I think, has expressed better the total correspondence our wills should have with God's will than the writer of the old litany of petitions called the "Universal Prayer." At one point it reads, "Volo quid vis, volo quia vis, volo quomodo vis, volo quamdiu vis." I translate it thus: "I want what you want. I want it because you want it. I want it in whatever way you want it. I want it for as long as you want it."

It is in this spirit that we address the first sorrowful mystery to our Father in heaven, in the name of Jesus Christ, true God yet truly our human brother, and aided by the intercession of Our Lady, who was also perfectly obedient to God.

THE SECOND SORROWFUL MYSTERY:
THE SCOURGING AT THE PILLAR

Seven centuries before the passion of Christ, Isaiah the prophet saw, as in a vision, a "Suffering Servant" sent to earth by God the Father. Isaiah quotes the Servant as declaring that he had been faithful to the divine command despite its pain: "I have not rebelled. I gave my back to those who beat me, my cheeks to those who plucked my beard; my face I did not shield from buffets and spitting" (50:5, 6).

That prediction was fulfilled when Pilate released Jesus into the hands of his executioners. He first had him scourged by some of his soldiers — a part of the ritual for those condemned to the cross. In so doing the soldiers added further abuses of their own (Mt 27:26; Mk 15:15; Lk 23:16; Jn19: 1-6).

Flagellation, Roman style, was a brutal torment that sometimes caused the death of the victim before he could be crucified. Stripped of his upper garment, the condemned man's hands were tied to a low column so that his bent back might feel the full effect of the blows. Two whippers used scourges made of leather strips with pieces of bone or lead affixed to their free ends so as to tear the skin to bits. The flow of blood was great, and the pain terrible. One of the most interesting aspects of the Holy Shroud of Turin is that it displays 100 wounds inflicted, on both the front and the back of the body, by whips of just this sort. It was after this traumatic experience that Pilate presented Our Lord to the populace, saying: "Ecce homo!" – "See your man!" Isaiah had also foretold this terrible sight: "Many were amazed by him – so marred was his look beyond that of mortals. There was in him no stately bearing to make us look at him, nor appearance that would attract us to him. A man of suffering . . . and we held him in no esteem. But he was pierced for our offenses, crushed for our sins; . . . by his stripes we were healed" (52-53).

Christ taught us not only by his actions but by the very sufferings he permitted be visited on him. Catholic piety has always understood this. We honor his Sacred Heart, for instance, as the wounded symbol of his redemptive love. We honor his "Sacred Head surrounded by crown of piercing thorn." We honor his Holy Face imprinted on the veil of Veronica.

We honor his Five Wounds. Should we not also honor the bloody welts of his scourging as making amends for the sensuality of fallen man?

Sensual sins are those that abuse our five God-given senses: sight, when we look at evil; hearing, when we listen to evil; smelling, when we inhale evil; taste, when we savor evil; touch, when we embrace evil. And sins of touch include not only sexual sins but the abuse of alcohol and drugs and other addictions; indeed, any tendency to make physical comfort and pleasure the be-all and end-all of life. Our Lord reminded his apostles of this constant human peril: "The spirit is willing but nature is weak" (Mt 26:41).

We should not be surprised, then, that throughout the Christian years saints and other devout souls, desiring to ward off sensual sins and atone for those committed, have made a practice of scourging themselves in token imitation of the scourging that Jesus submitted to on Good Friday. Devotional scourging is, of course, a problematic practice, not to be undertaken without the approval and guidance of our spiritual directors. For most of us the less extraordinary means of self-denial are safer: little mortifications of eyes, ears, nose, taste, and touch. In making them a part of our daily life we are joining Our Lord in putting weak, comfort-seeking nature in its place. We are doing penance for our own sensual frailties. We are also helping him to make reparation for the fleshly sins of others.

When we recite the second sorrowful mystery, let us offer our prayers as well for a world in which not love but self-indulgence has become for so many the rule of life. Let us say to Christ, "Thank you for submitting to so cruel a scourging. It has saved us from slavery to the flesh, for by your stripes we were healed."

THE THIRD SORROWFUL MYSTERY:
THE CROWNING WITH THORNS

Scourging was a prescribed part of the ritual of Roman crucifixions. Mockery was not. But Our Lord was also made the butt of insulting horseplay before being shouldered with his cross.

The Roman soldiers conducted their crude hazing not at the public site of the flagellation but within their own barracks, called the Praetorium. The whole cohort, numbering perhaps as many as 500-600 pagan military men, gathered to share in the fun.

Taking their cue from the title applied to Jesus, "the King of the Jews," which he himself did not reject, they decided to give him a burlesque coronation.

First they needed a robe of royal purple, so they tossed over his bleeding shoulders one of their red soldiers' cloaks. Next came the crown. Crowns worn by Roman emperors were not circlets of gold but wreaths of laurel leaves. But this king, the troops decided, deserved a more contemptuous tiara. So a couple of soldiers gingerly fashioned a sort of cap out of the twisted branches of a nearby thorn bush. As the Holy Shroud of Turin suggests, the thorns of this spiny cap pressed deep into the skin of the top as well as the brow, temples and back of the sacred head. Now only one symbol of sovereignty was missing, a scepter. For this a reed was plucked from the roadside and stuck into the bound hands of the Lord.

Then the militia paid mimic honors to this sad monarch. Approaching him as they would Caesar, they knelt and said, "Hail, King of the Jews!" But their sport was anything but deferential. They also slapped his face, spat on him, and even took his scepter and hit the crown with it so as to drive the briers still deeper into his head. The whole charade was a vicious atrocity. It ceased only when the command was given to start the procession to Calvary.

Two questions occur about this brutish comedy. The first is, what prompted the soldiers to perform it? The second, how did Jesus react to it?

The soldiers' motives were probably mixed. Pagan Romans in general disliked the Jews and their kings. Furthermore, those serving In the Roman army in Palestine were mostly pagan Palestinians and Syrians, known for their particular hostility to anything Jewish. One could, therefore, expect from none of the cohort a show of good will to any "King of the Jews." Perhaps the military also resented authority of any sort, and enjoyed taking out their resentment on Christ as a scapegoat of authority.

But I would especially see in their utter brutality that dark human vice that we have observed all too often in modern times: a cat-and-mouse tendency to dominate, to exercise power over somebody else. The Nazi SS were cruel to their prisoners because tyranny can be fun. The KGB, the ethnic cleansers of Yugoslavia, the warring tribes of Rwanda killed off their enemies because it settled antagonisms once and for all. Why do we suddenly have so many shootings in this country today? Is it not often because he who carries a gun can enjoy mastery over a multitude? Jesus had come to teach love, but men at their worst prefer to hate. In Jesus crowned with thorns, therefore, we have a stand-in for all those human beings whom the powerful have ever dehumanized.

And how did Jesus himself respond to his degraders? He simply accepted their insults, silently and without protest. He knew, as they did not, that they were fulfilling the prophecy of Isaiah about himself: "Though he was harshly treated, he submitted and opened not his mouth, like a lamb led to the slaughter or a sheep before the shearers" (53:7).

If Jesus suffered a crowning with thorns, can we not guess that he was inviting us to unite all our mental sufferings with his own? Countless thorns also stab into our own minds. The disregard and cruelty shown us by others. Nagging worries about our health and finances. Confusion in our times about the Church. Disappointment with our children, especially when they drift away from the faith or moral life. So many barbs, day after day! But look! Is his silent acceptance of interior pain intended to show us how to accept our own anguishes without opening our mouths? In joining our pain to his, are we not, in some small way, making reparation with him for all man's inhumanity to man?

As we pray the third sorrowful mystery, let us then say to our insulted King: O Sacred Head surrounded, by crown of piercing thorn; O bleeding Head so wounded, reviled and put to scorn: forgive us for ever having shown others mental cruelty; and help us to bear, with a patience like yours, the pains and heartaches of the mortal mind.

THE FOURTH SORROWFUL MYSTERY: THE CARRYING OF THE CROSS

"And when they had mocked him, they stripped him of the cloak, dressed him in his own clothes, and led him off to crucify him" (Mt 27:31).

The gospels give few details of Jesus' journey from the tribunal of Pilate to his place of execution, Skull Hill ("Calvary" in Latin, "Golgotha" in Aramaic). However, several of the details mentioned are significant.

For example, the carrying of the cross. St. John tells us that he was forced to bear it himself (19:17). It may have been a whole cross, or it may have been only the cross beam, to be attached to a post permanently standing on gallows hill. But the gospels of Matthew, Mark, and Luke add that (because, perhaps, of our Lord's weakness) the soldiers ordered a passerby to give Jesus a hand. All three evangelists say the man's name was Simon, identifying him as coming from Cyrene in North Africa. He was likely a member of the Jewish community in Cyrene who had come to Jerusalem as a pilgrim or to take up residence. Simon did not volunteer to bear the cross, therefore, but was commanded to do so by the military. In that sense he was a reluctant cooperator, as St. Alphonsus Liguori represents him in his famous meditations on the Stations of the Cross.

But there is reason to believe that the Cyrenian did not go unrewarded by our Savior for his assistance. The evangelists not only mention his name as a familiar one, but Mark adds that Simon was the father of Alexander and Rufus, as if the Romans for whom he wrote his gospel would recognize those two brothers. If that allusion did not imply that Simon himself later became a Christian, his sons quite likely did. A notable reward for the family of a man who had only grudgingly helped our Lord: the gift of grace! St. Paul was not the only beneficiary of Christ's superabundant generosity!

What was the attitude of the crowd that lined the Via Dolorosa?

When our Lord entered Jerusalem in modest but genuine triumph on Palm Sunday, accompanied by his Apostles, the people gave him royal honors. On Good Friday, however, he was hailed with no Hosannas. Even the Apostles, with the exception of young John, had taken to cowardly flight, among them Peter "the Rock" himself. There were, however, among those who watched Christ with pity some valiant women who had probably listened often to his golden words. When he saw them weeping, he paused for a moment to give them prophetic counsel. "Daughters of Jerusalem," he said tenderly, "do not weep for me; weep instead for yourselves and for your children." "For indeed," he warned, "the days are coming when people will say, 'Blessed are the barren, the wombs that never bore and the breasts that never nursed.' At that time people will say to the mountains, 'Fall upon us!' and to the hills, 'Cover us!' For if these things are done when the wood is green, what will happen when it is dry" (23:28-31)? In other words, if Jerusalem was today unjustly condemning the Just One – the vine that gives life – what punishment would be meted out to its citizens if they continued to be dry of faith? Quite likely, Jesus was here foretelling the hideous destruction of the city by the Romans in AD 70.

It is interesting to note that St. Luke speaks of the crowd not merely bystanding Jesus' procession but following him. Were they already fulfilling, even if unconsciously, his admonition, "If anyone wishes to come after me, he must deny himself and take up his cross and follow me" (Lk 9:23)?

The journey to Calvary was therefore tragic in that it represented the rejection of our Lord by the majority of those to whom he had preached daily in the temple. In the long run, however, it became for mankind a parable of salvation. Bearing his cross, he leads us on our pilgrimage to heaven, much as the pillar of fire led the Israelites in their desert journey from Egypt to the Promised Land. The famous medieval book *Imitation of Christ* opens with a similar thought: "I am the light of the world. Whoever follows me will not walk in darkness, but will have the light of life" (Jn 8:12). "These," it continues, "'are the words of Christ, by which we are admonished that we must imitate his life and manners, if we would be truly enlightened and delivered from all blindness of heart" (II, 1).

Vatican II spoke in the same vein when it referred to us as members of a Pilgrim Church. We trudge along in the present age towards our final goal. We march as members of a body that "carries the mark of this world which will pass." Yes, even the sacraments given to sustain us along the way are for this world and will be withdrawn from us in eternity as no longer necessary. Our journey is difficult, for we "groan and travail yet and await the revelation of the sons of God." Nevertheless, we march onward, utterly convinced that we are moving towards a new heaven and a new earth. That is why we pray to God in the Mass, "Strengthen in faith and love your pilgrim Church on earth!"

Thus, our Way of the Cross, like that of our Master, leads not only to death but to Resurrection. Wisely, then, does the *Imitation of Christ* observe, "If, indeed, there had been anything better and more beneficial to man's salvation than suffering, Christ would certainly have shown it by word and example" (II, XII, 15).

THE FIFTH SORROWFUL MYSTERY:
THE CRUCIFIXION

"Come, all you who pass by the way, look and see whether there is any suffering like my suffering."

These are the words put upon the lips of Zion -- that is, Jerusalem after the destruction of the Holy City in 587 BC, by the author of the Old Testament Book of Lamentations (1:12). The tragedy of Calvary was different from the fall of Jerusalem, but I can imagine Our Lady expressing the same lament as she witnessed the death of her Son on the cross. Let us try to look at the crucifixion through Mary's eyes.

Has God ever called on any other parent to both look on and consent to the sacrificial death of a deeply loved son? The only close parallel I can think of is the Patriarch Abraham and Jacob, his dear and only son and heir. The Book of Genesis records this touching story.

God had called Abraham out of Chaldea to Palestine to become the founder of the Israelites, his chosen people. Along the journey he elected to test Abraham's obedience. He therefore commanded him to take the boy to the Land of Moriah (where Jerusalem now stands) and offer him as a burned sacrifice.

As father and son neared the designated place, Abraham had Isaac shoulder the wood for the sacrificial fire, while he himself carried the firestone and the knife for the slaying. Thus far the parent had not told the boy what victim was to be offered up. So great was his grief that he could not bring himself to explain. But now the son was beginning to be suspicious. "Where is the sheep for the sacrifice?" he asked. Abraham could only say, "Son, God himself will provide the sheep for the holocaust."

Isaac's fears were confirmed when Abraham, having built a stone altar and laid the wood upon it, sadly bound the boy, lifted him up onto the pyre, and raised the knife to slay his beloved child. But at that very moment God sent an angel to stay the execution: "I know now how devoted you are to God, since you did not withhold your own beloved son." Catching sight of a ram caught in the underbrush, the obedient Patriarch offered that instead and the genealogy of Jesus was not interrupted. God had indeed provided the sacrificial sheep.

Was Mary's sorrow on Mount Calvary any greater than Abraham's on Mount Moriah? She, too, had been given a precious son. Warned from the beginning that her heart would be pierced by a sword of sorrow because of this son, she had nevertheless obediently consented to God's plan that he be offered in sacrifice. Like Abraham, Mary also walked with her child to the place of his execution. But Mary's grief differed from Abraham's in one major way. At the end, God sent the Patriarch a substitute victim. In the case of Our Lady, there was no substitute. The victim offered was and could only be the very Lamb of God. God demanded of Mary this still more radical obedience, to ratify the total obedience of Jesus himself. Furthermore, the stakes were far more important than in Abraham's case. Only by the death of the God-man could the disobedience of Adam be atoned for and fallen mankind be redeemed. As Jesus bowed to the will of the Father, to become a second and better Adam, so Mary bowed to the will of the Father, to become a second and better Eve.

It is painful to have to watch others suffer and be unable to help them. Jesus had doubtless foreseen each aspect of his agony. Perhaps Mary, too, had been informed by God in advance of the program of his passion. Some artists and writers have imagined that Our Lady swooned at the foot of the cross. Not at all. That would have permitted her to forget momentarily her own duty of moral support. As Jesus refused any anesthetic (the wine flavored with gall), so she refused to faint. St. John writes clearly that Mary was "standing by the cross of Jesus" (19: 25). As the well-known hymn says, "Stabat Mater Dolorosa / Iuxta Crucem lacrymosa, Dum pendebat Filius . . ." "At the Cross her station keeping / stood the mournful Mother weeping / Close to Jesus to the last." Christ could have saved us by shedding one drop of his blood, but he gave all. His mother, too, gave the full measure of her compassion. His last words were, "It is finished." Her last comment was silent acceptance. Who has expressed this acceptance better than the sculptor Michelangelo in his great statue the Pieta? Seated with the limp body of her dead Son on her lap, Mary lowers her eyes, and although there is inexpressible sadness on her lips, she holds out her hand in a gesture of perfect resignation. At the Annunciation she had replied to the Archangel, "Behold, I am the handmaid of the Lord. May it be done to me according to your word" (Lk 1:38). Now her whole attitude at the conclusion of Christ's passion and her own compassion can be summarized by the word "Amen."

We were saved by Christ's sacrifice on Calvary. The crucifix is the constant symbol of that salvation. Let us recall that fact every time we bless ourselves. At every Mass, too, the saving passion is re-presented in an unbloody manner. Let us always unite ourselves with that self-sacrifice. And when the priest raises chalice and host and proclaims "Through him, with him, in him in the unity of the Holy Spirit, all glory and honor is yours, almighty Father, for ever and ever," let us cry out in thanks with Mary: Amen. So be it. Amen!

THE FIRST GLORIOUS MYSTERY:
THE RESURRECTION

"This is the day the Lord has made; let us be glad and rejoice in it" (Ps 118:24).

We recognize these words as used in the liturgy of Easter. The original comes from Psalm 118. It seems to have been written to commemorate a stunning earthly victory, but its verses fit in sublimely with Jesus' resurrection. Indeed, the following verse cries out, "O Lord, grant salvation," which in Hebrew is "Hosanna." And the Hebrew of "This is the day the Lord has made" is actually "This is the day the Lord has acted," that is, God the Father "raised him from the dead," as St. Paul says. "Believe this in your heart," Paul assures us, and "you will be saved" (Rom 10:9).

The death of Christ on the cross was absolutely necessary for our redemption. Without the passion of him who was God as well as man, reparation could not have been made to God for that sin of Adam that had lost for his descendants the friendship of their Creator. But the resurrection of Christ was also absolutely necessary to confirm our redemption and to guarantee our own resurrection. As St. Paul told the Corinthians, "If Christ has not been raised, your faith is in vain, you are still in your sins" (I Cor 15:17). In his raising we read the promise of our own.

It is interesting to see just how Christ revealed his resurrection, the great proof of his victory over death and of his complete power over all creation. When he preached, that was a public act, as were most of his miracles. When he suffered and died, that was a public act, and was intended to be. Hundreds heard his sermons and saw his healings; hundreds watched his execution. When he rose from the dead, however, it was in secret: as the poet put it, "alone, alone, behind the stone." One can only begin to imagine the purely human emotions that were his when his soul, having visited Limbo and announced salvation to the worthy dead, reassumed his human body, and Christ, revived, felt again the joyous beat of his human heart. Then he stood up from the cold stone slab, doffed his winding-cloths, and with the agility characteristic of a risen body, passed through the stone that closed off his sepulcher. Angels then rolled away the great stone so that those who would soon seek Jesus' remains might see the empty tomb. He himself had already gone where he would, now in that glorified humanity that permits one to appear or disappear at will before human eyes, or to fly at will from place to place in the universe.

The accounts of Jesus after the resurrection, as given in the New Testament, are full of this mysterious glory. How he spent the next forty days in general we do not know. It is a reasonable conjecture that the first person he visited in his new life was his own dear mother. Then he returned to the tomb and chose to reveal himself to St. Mary Magdalen: teasingly, for at first she did not recognize him. Next he appeared to his apostles, fearfully locked into the upper chamber (Jn 20). To prove that it was really himself in the flesh, he ate a piece of fish (Lk 24:42). Then he joined the two disciples bound for Emmaus, and showed them his identity at suppertime, at the breaking of bread (Lk 24). A week later he joined the apostles once more in the Cenacle, and now won the recognition of St. Thomas, who had been absent on Easter Sunday. "My Lord and my God," Thomas exclaimed, finally convinced. Jesus replied, "Blessed are those who have not seen and have believed" (Jn 20: 29).

Sometime later Jesus appeared in Galilee. Now the crowd was large, but still restricted to his own followers. He made it possible for the apostles to catch another miraculous draft of fishes in the Sea of Galilee, and then gave them fish to eat on its shore. They did not ask him who he was, but they knew it was indeed he, though marvelously changed.

Why did our Lord act so mysteriously after rising from the dead? I think to emphasize that although still human as well as divine, he now wanted them to realize that he was more than ever of the next world. And why did he appear only to his chosen followers? Was it not to emphasize that he had finished his earthly mission and would now leave his task in the hands of those whom he had taught, to be guided henceforth by the Holy Spirit?

Through the death and resurrection of Jesus, therefore, we have been saved. By baptism we are already sons of God and heirs of heaven, but our own resurrection is not yet realized. He wants us to forge ahead, loyal to the teachings of the Gospel passed on to us by the successors of his apostles. I am sure that we often envy a little the original disciples of our Lord. Wouldn't it have been wonderful to listen to Jesus with our own ears, to take part in the Last Supper, to shed our own tears at his crucifixion, and to rejoice in his resurrection? Yes, his first followers were indeed blessed. But no more blessed than we are. The presence of the living Christ was not enough to convert his listeners. They had to make an act of faith in his divinity just as we do, and many did not go that far. Even St. Thomas doubted the resurrection. No, we are just as fortunate as the disciples, despite being late-comers. We hear Jesus preach through the scriptures and the teaching voice of the Church, and we know that the Holy Spirit preserves his doctrine unchanged. And although he is absent from our eyes, he is present to us always in the Holy Eucharist, renewing each day, through the words of the priest, his passion, death, resurrection and ascension. Like the two disciples bound for Emmaus on Easter Day, we recognize him in the "breaking of bread" (Lk 24:35). Like St. Thomas the Apostle we hail in faith the risen Christ, "My Lord and my God!" (Jn 20:28)

THE SECOND GLORIOUS MYSTERY:
THE ASCENSION

"He ascended into heaven." In these words, which appear In both the Apostles' Creed and the Creed of Nicaea, we proclaim our belief that after his resurrection our Lord returned to the heaven he had left at the Incarnation, bringing with him the body and soul of a human being. What the two creeds proclaim is, of course, set down in the gospels (Mk 16:19, Lk 24:51). St. Luke also describes the event in the Acts of the Apostles (Chapter 1).

At their last gathering, the Apostles had asked Jesus when the kingdom of Israel was to be reestablished. They apparently still thought that his kingdom would be political. Our Lord bypassed the question by replying that the Father alone could give the answer. Now, however, they should wait in Jerusalem for the arrival of the Holy Spirit. With him as guide they would carry the good news of the redemption to the end of the earth.

When he had said this, the Acts of the Apostles continues, "Jesus was lifted up and a cloud took him from their sight" (Acts 1:9). A cloud was here on the Mount of Olives, as it had been on Mount Sinai, a signal of the divine presence. Despite his disappearance, the Eleven kept looking up forlornly, until "suddenly two men dressed in white garments stood beside them." "Men of Galilee," said these angels (for such they were), "why are you standing there looking at the sky? This Jesus, who has been taken up from you to heaven, will return in the same way as you have seen him going into heaven." In other words, go now about your business. Do whatever he told you to do.

As you will recall, Mary had given the same advice to the servants at the wedding feast of Cana ("Do whatever he tells you") just prior to his first miracle. Each one of us has been given a certain role to perform in life, just as the musician is assigned a special part to play in a symphony orchestra. If we fail to play our part in the symphony of life, all creation is in discord. If we play it well, we will merit the standing ovation of heaven. So it is our responsibility not to shirk or lollygag, but to do what we should, when we should and how we should. As Franklin D. Roosevelt once said in another context, "Never . . . have we had so little time in which to do so much."

Not that the task of the moment is always a heavy one. The young Jesuit saint John Berchmans found fidelity to duty the secret of holiness. At one time when the rule for his fellow novices said they should spend an hour at recreation, he joined in a game of billiards. During the match, a thoughtful fellow player asked him, "If the end of the world should come right now, what would you do?" "I'd keep playing billiards," he replied. In other words, he would continue doing what he was supposed to do.

This one aspect of the ascension of Christ, the reminder to be about our business, is especially relevant today, when the Church founded by Christ on the Apostles, and given the protection of the Holy Spirit, seems to be facing ever more problems. What are we going to do about them?

Recently an anguished young Catholic woman asked me, "What is going to happen to the Church?" I had no specific advice to give, but I volunteered what I think is a valid answer: "I don't know what's going to happen exactly. What I do know is that Christ founded his church, and it is his business to keep it going. And I firmly believe that in his own good time he will straighten things out."

What we are called on to do, then, in these times as well as all times, is whatever our faith and our circumstances tell us to do from hour to hour. That is, again, to be about our business and leave the worrying to God. After all, what else did the Apostles do after Our Lord's ascension? Obeying the angel, they set about spreading the Gospel. It was a hard task, but see how it finally turned out. They established the Church.

In one of his parables, Jesus warned: Don't be like servants who misbehave and fritter away time when their master goes traveling. He may return suddenly and ask for an accounting, and woe to the delinquent servant: "Much will be required of the person entrusted with much."

Let us then serve our Master diligently, "doing whatever he has told us" until he reappears for the reckoning. Then, when he who was swept up into heaven on Ascension Day returns in the flesh to earth, now in power and glory, he will conduct us up with him into the eternal wedding feast, as his "good and faithful servants."

THE THIRD GLORIOUS MYSTERY:
THE DESCENT OF THE HOLY SPIRIT

In one of his witty novels, the English Catholic writer Hilaire Belloc recounted a theological conversation on a British train between a Catholic and a blustery agnostic. They were speaking of the Holy Spirit. "What makes me mad," stormed the agnostic, "is all this talk about the Holy Ghost, the Holy Ghost. They might at least show a picture of him in the newspapers, but no, just talk, talk!"

You and I know perfectly well why the swarm of paparazzi doesn't wing after the Holy Spirit to snap him for the tabloids, or the TV cameramen don't focus on him for their news broadcasts. He is a spirit, a pure spirit, and no spirit can be seen by bodily eyes, much less captured on film. Only twice has the Holy Ghost permitted himself to be seen physically, and then it was in symbol; as a dove from heaven at the baptism of Our Lord, and as diverse tongues of flame at Pentecost.

In a way, it is regrettable that we are not allowed to see him, for he plays a major part in our lives. On the other hand, even if as a result of his modesty he is the most easily forgotten person of the Holy Trinity, it is probably best that he operate in secret. "Love makes the world go round," says the familiar proverb, but have you ever seen a photo of Love? The Holy Spirit is the spirit of love, bent on captivating not our eyes but our hearts.

When Jesus ascended into heaven, his disciples grieved to have him depart: he had become their teacher, guide, and defender. Aware of their affection, he had promised, "I will not leave you orphans" (Jn 14:18). His Father would send them, he said, another "advocate," another "Paraclete" to be with them always (Jn 14:16). "He will teach you everything and remind you of all that I told you" (Jn 14:25).

That promise was kept on Pentecost Sunday. When the disciples were still huddled together in the Cenacle, the sound of a wind roared in, filling the whole house. In Hebrew, the word for wind and spirit is the same. Like our own climatic winds that blow strong when a high-pressure system is taking over, this wind-sound was a symbol of a change to come, a divine change. Then tongues of flickering flame appeared hovering in the air above them, parted and came to rest on the heads of each one of them, and they were filled with the Holy Spirit, speaking in different tongues.

Centuries before, God had signaled his presence to Moses in the burning bush on Mount Sinai, in preparation for the old covenant between God and man. These fiery tongues of Pentecost indicated the inauguration of the new covenant (Acts, Ch. 2).

Up to this point, the disciples had been practically in hiding, fearful that they, too, might be arrested and punished because they had been partisans of Jesus. The Holy Spirit changed all that in a split second. Inspired by a sudden courage that did not count the cost, Christ's followers unbarred the door and poured out into the streets, boldly preaching to all they met about the crucified Messiah. And the Spirit opened the ears of their listeners and made them heed the new message. "What must we do to be saved?" they asked in great earnest. Peter answered, "Repent and be baptized, every one of you, in the name of Jesus Christ, for the forgiveness of your sins, and you will receive the gift of the Holy Spirit." They did repent. They did ask for baptism. That day 3,000 received the Holy Ghost through baptism in the name of the Father and of the Son and of the Holy Spirit (Acts, Ch. 2).

The ancient Fathers of the Church used to say that the Church was born on Calvary from the pierced side of Christ, the Second Adam, much as Eve was brought into being from the side of the First Adam. But if the Church's birth is to be dated from Good Friday, can we not say that its birthday celebration was on Pentecost? Then the Spirit solemnly entered the new Church to become its soul, to remain its ruler, its instructor, and its sanctifier. He hallowed the individuals baptized as he would do forever after at baptism, kindling in them the fire of his love.

The Spirit not only makes us holy through sanctifying grace, but brings us countless gifts as well. The prophet Isaiah listed the chief gifts, which, if cultivated, will make us true reflections of God himself. There is Wisdom (that is, enlightened common sense). There is Understanding (that is, a ready grasp of divine truth). There is Counsel (that is, a practical prudence). There is Fortitude (that is, strength of character.) There is Knowledge (that is, an intuition of how whatever happens relates to eternity). There is Fear of the Lord or Piety (that is, a wholesome fear of doing anything that would offend our Father in heaven.)

Every good tree bears good fruit, Our Lord said, and every rotten tree bears rotten fruit. "So, by their fruits you will know them" (Mt 7:20). St.

Paul lists some of the good fruits that the Holy Spirit causes the good soul to produce. "The fruit of the Spirit," he says, "is love, joy, peace, patience, kindness, generosity, faithfulness, gentleness, and self-control" (Gal 5:22-23). Just think for a moment of the people, living or dead, whom you hold in the highest regard. Are they not persons who bear, precisely, these rich fruits? And do they not bear them, precisely, because they cultivate to the best of their ability the various gifts of the Holy Spirit? If all men and women were as heedful as those whom you consider heroes, would there not be an end to injustice, violence, and war in the world?

When we received the Holy Ghost in baptism, it was the most important event in our spiritual lives. Since then, the Spirit has constantly channeled into our souls the gifts of the Father through the mediation of the Son. How much we owe, then, to this self-effacing member of the Holy Trinity! How carefully should we heed St. Paul's warning: "Do not grieve the Holy Spirit of God, with which you were sealed for the day of redemption" (Eph. 4:30).

St. John of Damascus composed a prayer that we might well make our own:

> Lead me to pastures. Lord, and graze there with me. Do not let my heart lean either to the right or the left, but let your good Spirit guide me along the straight path. Whatever I do, let it be in accordance with your will, now and forever. Amen.

THE FOURTH GLORIOUS MYSTERY: THE ASSUMPTION

The death of Our Lord on Calvary grieved his mother in yet another way. It marked the beginning of a separation of a parent and child whose earthly lives had been intimately associated since the day of the annunciation. As we have seen, Jesus, after his resurrection, most likely appeared to Mary, consoling her with the knowledge that he had risen from the dead. Nevertheless, after his ascension, Our Lady and he would never enjoy perfect togetherness anymore until she, too, had lived out her earthly life.

Jesus on Calvary had entrusted Mary to the care of St. John the Apostle, and he surely discharged this duty conscientiously. Apart from indicating that the Blessed Mother was held in high reverence by all Christ's disciples, the Scriptures give us precious few data about her own life. We are told nothing about her immaculate conception. We are told nothing about her later life and her assumption: nothing, that is, except that the Archangel Gabriel hailed her with the profound greeting "Hail, full of grace." Profound, I say, because both the dogma of her immaculate conception and her assumption are founded on Gabriel's words.

Christ revealed more, however, than is recorded in the bible. Other truths were communicated to the Church by tradition, and every now and then the official teachers of the Church have declared that one or another of these unwritten truths are a part of the deposit of our faith.

By the fifth century it is quite clear that Christians believed that at her life's end Our Lady was taken up into heaven, body and soul. Thus in the sixth century, the French bishop St. Gregory wrote that Christ himself came down and took Mary's soul to heaven and on the next day her body (Jurgens 2288a). In the eighth century, St. John of Damascus wrote that in assuming her into heaven, God intended to honor her immaculate body with a resurrection that anticipated the general resurrection (Jurgens 2390). Nor were SS. Gregory and John of Damascus spinning fantasies. What they said reflected earlier tradition. Church artists in both east and west began at least in the ninth century to depict Mary's ascent into heaven. And at least by AD 500, a special feast day in the Mideast honored this Falling Asleep (Dormition) of Our Lady. Rome accepted the feast in the seventh century but gave it the title Assumption of Mary. It was long the main Marian feast day.

The Holy See formally accepted a Feast of the Immaculate Conception in 1476. In 1854, Pope Pius IX, having consulted with all the Catholic bishops of the world on their teaching that Mary was conceived free from original sin, concluded that this doctrine was a matter of Catholic faith. Therefore, the Pope defined the Immaculate Conception as a dogma. Pope Pius XII, again after consulting with his fellow bishops about Mary's Assumption, found that they confirmed his own belief in the doctrine, and in 1950 solemnly confirmed the Assumption as a dogma of faith. The exact words of the Pope's definition were: "The Immaculate Mother of God, the ever-Virgin Mary, having completed the course of her earthly life, was assumed body and soul into heavenly glory."

That Our Lady should have been taken up to heaven, body and soul alike, was entirely appropriate. Jesus, who shared our human nature in all but sin, obtained his human flesh from his mother, who was likewise, through divine grace, free from all stain of sin, original or actual. Although her role in the redemption was subordinate to his, she was associated with him in that achievement as nobody else was. It was her consent to God that made her divine motherhood possible. It was she who gave birth to the Messiah in the stable of Bethlehem. It was she who presented him at the temple and raised him in the art of living. It was she who prompted him to perform his first miracle. It was she who stood by the cross on which he died, and accepted from him the foster-motherhood of St. John the Apostle, and through that commission, the motherhood of the whole Church. It was she who, from Pentecost onward, was cherished by all the faithful as the dear remembrancer of his teachings. Did she not deserve from God himself a special reward for her role as "co-redemptress"?

As early as the year AD 155, St. Justin the Martyr had declared that Mary deserved the title "the Second Eve." God had created the First Adam and the First Eve sinless, and commanded them to people and develop the world. But they had fallen into sin and out of friendship with their Creator. At length, God himself would repair the breach, for he alone could. He sent a Second Adam, Christ, the God-Man, to heal the wound by his death on the cross. And his elect mother, a human being conceived without original sin, would assist Jesus to begin all over again to create a People of

God. The Second Adam rose from his redeeming death and ascended body and soul into heaven. It was fitting that his principal associate, the Second Eve, should also be taken early to heaven. Not only can she continue in heaven her intercession with Jesus on behalf of us her children. She remains for us likewise a constant reminder that as she now is, so will we be, when we rise from dust into new life, and stand body and soul before the eternal majesty of God.

Therefore when we meditate on this mystery of the Assumption, we anticipate our own resurrection, and we pray that not only ourselves but all our brothers and sisters may rise into the glory that our Mother wants so much to share with us.

THE FIFTH GLORIOUS MYSTERY:
MARY IS CROWNED QUEEN OF HEAVEN

As citizens of a democratic republic we reject rule by kings or queens. But we know enough about the concept of a single ruler to appreciate the title given to Jesus in the bible, "King of kings and Lord of lords."

We can also appreciate the fitness of calling Mary a queen. Scripture may not refer to her thus in so many words, but it lays the basis for the practice. The Archangel Gabriel himself, in announcing that Our Lord would be born of her, said that Jesus "will be called Son of the Most High, and the Lord God will give him the throne of David his father, and he will rule over the house of Jacob forever, and of his kingdom there will be no end" (Lk 1:32-33). If the child of her consent would be of royal status without end, she herself would be of royal status without end.

Mary would not of course be the reigning monarch of God's kingdom as Maria Teresa was ruler of Austria, or Catherine the Great was ruler of Russia, or Elizabeth I was ruler of England. She would be instead a "queen mother," much as St. Helena was the honored queen mother of Roman emperor Constantine. In fact, St. Elizabeth practically called Mary that, when at the Visitation she exclaimed, "And how does this happen to me, that the mother of my Lord should come to me" (Lk 1:43)? The term "mother of the Lord" in Hebrew means just that. A queen mother may not rule, but she is in a unique position to put in a good word for others with her monarch child. The British monarchy in the latter half of the twentieth century provides a good illustration of such influence. If Queen Elizabeth II discharged her duties with dignity, the younger members of the House of Windsor often behaved "unroyally." Through it all, one "royal" who continued in high esteem because of her good example was the widow of King George VI, Queen Mother Elizabeth, fondly known by Britons as the "Queen Mum."

Queen Mother Mary has far more notable credentials than the Windsor dynasty, and infinitely greater influence. Like her divine Son, she owes her rank to two factors. First, her Son by family descent was heir to his ancestor King David. Second, Jesus' kingship was merited by conquest as well as by descent. By his own death he had conquered death itself. As he told the Apostles, "In the world you will have troubles, but take courage, I have conquered the world" (Jn 16:33). Mary, both by family descent and by her own cooperation with her Son in the Redemption, was qualified to play a greater role than any other human being in the governance of the renewed human race.

What is the nature of her governance?

An actual ruler has the triple power of lawgiver, executive, and judge. Our Lady enjoys these powers only by delegation, and then within limitations. We can scarcely think of her as judge, for instance, since a judge must punish, and who can think of Mary as a punisher? No, her mission is basically that of a go-between, a mediator. Not a mediator between man and God. That is the function of Christ alone. But a mediator, or more precisely, a mediatrix to heed the prayers of her human children, pass them on to her Son, and at times play a personal role in their fulfillment. Mary the Queen, in other words, is still the Mary who at Cana persuaded Christ to perform his first miracle; not, remember, because the newlyweds had even asked for it, but simply because in her motherly heart she saw that it would be a gracious and timely deed.

In pondering the fifth glorious mystery, should we try to visualize the crowning of the Queen of Heaven as artists have depicted it, a heavenly liturgy in which Father, Son, and Holy Spirit confer a glittering tiara on the Blessed Virgin? This is artistic fantasy, but the Scriptures do allude to her royal status in heaven. Psalm 45 was perhaps prophetic when it sang, "The Queen takes her place at your right hand in gold of Ophir" (v. 10). And the Book of Revelation shows the vision of "a woman clothed with the sun, with the moon under her feet, and on her head a crown of twelve stars" (Apoc. 12:1).

Christian devotion has never hesitated to proclaim the nobility of Mary of Nazareth by calling her "Lady:" "Our Lady Notre Dame," "Nostra Signora," "Nuestra Señora," "Panna Maria," and so forth; these all say the same thing. And think of the regal titles that we bestow lavishly on the mother of the King of Kings: "Queen of Heaven," Queen of Angels," "Queen of All Saints," "Queen, Beauty of Carmel," "Queen Conceived without Original Sin," "Queen of the Holy Rosary," "Queen of Families," "Queen of Peace."

It is wonderful for us to have, seated at the right hand of the Father, a King of Kings who shares our human nature. It is also wonderful for us to have, seated at the right hand of her Son, an ever watchful "Queen Mum" to tell him when we run out of wine.

Curriculum Vitae

2001

REV. ROBERT FRANCIS McNAMARA

Born in Corning Hospital, Corning, NY, November 3, 1910, to Thomas A. McNamara, M.D., and Helen Dwyer McNamara. Raised in St. Mary's Parish, Corning. Attended St. Mary's School, 1916-1924, and Corning Free Academy, 1924-1928. Attended Georgetown University, Washington, DC, 1928-1932, graduating with an A.B. in 1932. Attended Harvard University School of Arts and Sciences 1932-1933 and received the degree A.M. in 1933.

Adopted as a candidate for the priesthood by the Diocese of Rochester, NY, in 1933, he entered the North American College, Rome, Italy, a residence for American diocesan seminarians enrolled at the Pontifical Gregorian University. Awarded the S.T.L., (Licentiate of Sacred Theology), July 1937. He was ordained to the priesthood in Rome on December 8, 1936, by the vicar general of the diocese of Rome, Cardinal Francesco Marchetti-Selvaggiani.

Returning to the United States in summer 1937, he was named assistant pastor of St. Francis Xavier Church in Rochester, assigned to work especially among Italians at the Chapel of the Annunciation in Rochester. In June 1938 he was appointed to the editorial staff of the Rochester diocesan newspaper, the *Catholic Courier Journal,* and concurrently chaplain of St. Ann's Home, Lake Avenue, Rochester, NY. In September 1938, however, he was appointed to the faculty of the diocesan major seminary, St. Bernard's, at 2260 Lake Avenue, to teach Church history. Father McNamara continued at that post until 1981, when the seminary closed. In due time he was promoted to the rank of Full Professor of Church History; but he also taught, at various times, patrology, liturgy, and Italian. In the spring semesters of 1972 and 1976, he was Visiting Professor of U.S. Catholic History at the Toronto School of Theology at Toronto, Ont., Canada. His additional writings and lectures included local secular history as well as ecclesiastical history. His interest in art history was reflected not only in his course of seminary lectures on religious art but also in other writings and activities.

Professor McNamara has been a member of the following professional societies: American Historical Association; N.Y. State Historical Association; American Association for State and Local History; Society of American Archivists; American Society of Church History. He was a founder and first president of the Corning-Painted Post, NY, Historical Society (1947); also second vice-president of the American Catholic Historical Association (1970) and advisory editor of its *Catholic Historical Review* (1948-1955). He was likewise a member of The Liturgical Arts Society, Inc., and a member of its board (1959-1972).

In addition to priestly service in his diocese, Fr. McNamara served on several committees, including the diocesan Liturgical Commission (1965-1976). He was appointed diocesan archivist in 1976, and reappointed in 1996.

WRITINGS: Father McNamara's many booklets and articles have been principally historical, dealing with secular as well as Catholic history. He contributed to the following works of reference: *New Catholic Encyclopedia* (1967); *Dictionnaire d'histoire et de géographie écclésiastiques* (1963); *Catholic Encyclopedia for School and Home* (1965); *Dictionary of Christianity in America* (1990); *Encyclopedia of American Catholic History* (1997).

Editorial
Co-editor: Alexander M. Stewart, *French Pioneers in the Eastern Great Lakes Area, 1609-1791* (1970). Editor: *Essays in Honor of Joseph P. Brennan* (1976).

Local History items for Rochester area
Major Carroll: "Charles Carroll of Belle Vue, Co-founder of Rochester," *Rochester History*, 1980; "In Search of the Carrolls of Belle Vue," *Maryland Historical Magazine*, 1985; "John Carroll and Interfaith Marriages: The Case of the Carrolls of Belle Vue," in Minnich/Eno/ Trisco, *Studies in Catholic History in Honor of John Tracy Ellis* (1985).
Col. William Fitzhugh: "William Frisby Fitzhugh, Co-founder of Rochester," pub. Rochester Historical Society, 1984.

Other Rochesteriana
"Archbishop Hanna, Rochesterian," *Rochester History*, 1963; "Ecumenism and the Rochester Center for Theological Studies," *Rochester History*, 1990.

Southern Tier, N.Y. items
Jack Mack; or The Shooting of Ellen Callinan, A Forgotten Corning Tragedy (1990). "Old-Style Family Physician, Corning's 'Doc Mac' (1856-1927)," serialized in *The Crooked Lake Review* (Hammondsport, NY, issues 35-37, 1991).

Parish Bulletin articles (St. Thomas the Apostle Church, Rochester, NY) "All God's Children," 1981-1984 (syndicated by Parish Publications, Inc., 1984). "Saints Alive," 1984 to present (syndicated by Parish Publications, Inc., as "Saints Go Marching," 1988-1990).

BOOKS
A Century of Grace: A History of St. Mary's Roman Catholic Parish, Corning, N.Y., 1848-1948. Corning, NY: 1948, 1979.

The American College in Rome, 1855-1955. Rochester, NY: 1956.

The Diocese of Rochester, 1868-1968. Rochester, NY: 1968.

St. Bernard's Seminary, 1893-1968. Rochester, NY: 1968.

Catholic Sunday Preaching: The American Guidelines, 1791-1975, Washington, DC: 1976.

Ambassadors for Christ: A Necrology of Priests and Permanent Deacons Who Have Served Within the Diocese of Rochester-in-America, 1818-1993. Rochester, NY: 1994.

The Diocese of Rochester in America, 1868-1993 (second edition, amended and updated to the Diocese's 125th year). Rochester, NY: 1998.

DISTINCTIONS

Olcott Medal, Corning Free Academy, 1928; Lynch-Pendergast Medal, Georgetown University, 1932; (Hon.) Doctorate of Divinity, St. Bernard's Seminary, 1981; (Hon.) Doctorate of Humane Letters, St. John Fisher College, Rochester, NY, 1985. Initial recipient of the Founders' Medal of the Pontifical North American College, Rome, 1990. Inducted into Steuben County (NY) Hall of Fame, 1991. Initial recipient, President's Award, St. Bernard's Institute, 1998.

SOME NOTES ON A FEW OF MY UNDERTAKINGS

Professor of Church History, St. Bernard's Seminary, 1938-1981.

In addition to a number of parish histories, plus newspaper articles, reviews, letters to editors, etc., I list what are the more important productions over the years:

Books

A Century of Grace, written about and published by my home parish, St. Mary's, Corning, in commemoration of the parish centenary. First edition, 1948. Reprint, 1979. "A valuable source for New York religious and social history": Wendell Tripp, *New York History*, LXXI, 344-45.

The American College in Rome, 1855-1955 (Rochester, 1956). An 800-page study of my Roman Alma Mater. "Will find an enduring place in the literature of the American Church": John Tracy Ellis, *America*, January 26, 1957; "An interesting venture into this fascinating chapter of American Church history": J. Risk, S.J., in *Gregorianum* (Rome) XL 4, 1959; "Holds the interest from start to finish; a model in this type of study": Roger Aubert, in *Revue D'Histoire Ecclesiastique* (Louvain), January 1958, No. 1, 229-30.

The Diocese of Rochester, 1868-1968 (Rochester, 1968). First edition.

Ambassadors for Christ: A Necrology of Priests and Permanent Deacons Who Have Served Within the Diocese of Rochester-in-America, 1818-1993. Paperback published by the Archives, Diocese of Rochester, 1994. (This necrology, twice corrected and updated since 1994, lists dates of death in the calendared section. In the biographical section the same names are listed alphabetically, with dates of birth, religious profession, and ordination to the extent that the data are available. (Cited by Wendell Tripp, *New York History*, July 1997, LXXVII, 358.)

St. Bernard's Seminary, 1893-1968. This is the 1968 issue of *The Sheaf,* annual of St. Bernard's Seminary, 1954-1981. Although written in popular style it is the only history of the seminary ever attempted.

Articles: General

I have written and published articles and reviews on general historical, liturgical, and canonical subjects in a number of periodicals, among which are: *The Catholic World, The Catholic Historical Review, America, Records of the Catholic Historical Society* (Philadelphia), *Ecclesia* (Vatican), *Ave Maria, Jubilee, The Priest, The Ecclesiastical Review, The Homiletic and Pastoral Review, The Americas, New York History, Revue D'Histoire Ecclesiastique, Liturgical Arts, Historical Records and Studies* (U.S. Catholic Historical Society), *Continuum, Moreana* (Angers, France), *The Tablet* (London), *Upstate Magazine* (Rochester), *The Maryland Historical Magazine* (Baltimore), *The Canadian Catholic Review.*

Articles in Encyclopedias

Dictionnaire D'Histoire Et De Geographie Ecclesiastique (Paris), 1963; *Catholic Encyclopedia for School and Home,* 1965; *New Catholic Encyclopedia,* 1967; *Dictionary of Christianity in America,* 1990; *Encyclopedia of American Catholic History,* 1997.

Articles on Rochester Area History

The Catholic Courier, published by the Diocese of Rochester under that and other titles, has often opened its columns to my manuscripts since the time that I was its assistant editor in 1938. Probably the most significant of these articles were those on Rochester and the Civil War (the 1960s particularly, but others at later dates), and my articles on the art and architecture of various diocesan church buildings.

Rochester's Co-founders *

I am deeply gratified to have been able to provide something that nobody had attempted before: brief but researched articles on the lives of Rochester's two co-founders, Major Charles Carroll of Belle Vue and Col. William Fitzhugh. My study of Carroll ("Charles Carroll of Belle Vue, Co-founder of Rochester") was published by *Rochester History* in 1980. Thanks to the gracious interest of Elizabeth Holahan of the Rochester Historical Society, my "William Frisby Fitzhugh, Co-founder of Rochester" was published in 1984 by the Rochester Historical Society in a splendid typographical format.

I have given St. John Fisher Library, for their archive of Rochesteriana, all my papers dealing with these two projects. I wanted to express in some concrete manner my gratitude to the college for bestowing on me the honorary degree of L.H.D. in 1984.

* Nathaniel Rochester, Rochester's founder, had honored his co-founders (who settled in Groveland) by attaching their names to two streets. After the death of Col. Rochester and Charles Carroll, the Rochester government, as the result of a disagreement with Charles Holker Carroll, Major Carroll's heir, over some local property rights, erased the name Carroll from the 100-acre plot and renamed it State Street. This was generally denounced as an act of vengeance for over a century but nothing

was done about it. Only in the late 1900s did Mayor Stephen May promote the restoration of the Carroll name to the riverbank park facility that was eventually named Major Charles Carroll Plaza in memory of the co-founder. I was happy to help the mayor in this project, and my article was largely inspired by his efforts.

Rochester History also published two other articles from my pen.

The first one dealt with a Rochester priest, Rev. Dr. Edward J. Hanna, who was a native Rochesterian, taught theology at St. Bernard's Seminary, was prominent in social causes in the city, and eventually became archbishop of San Francisco. "Archbishop Hanna, Rochesterian," appeared in *Rochester History* 25 (1963).

My last contribution to this publication appeared in Fall 1990, Vol. LII: "Ecumenism and the Rochester Center for Theological Studies." This essay recorded the establishment of a Catholic/Protestant/Anglican consortium participated in by Colgate Rochester Divinity School, St. Bernard's Seminary, Bexley Hall, and Crozer Divinity School. To this interesting undertaking, which I saw as a fruit of the growth of the ecumenical spirit in the Rochester area after the Second Vatican Council, the moving of St. Bernard's graduate department to "The Hill" after the closing of St. Bernard's Seminary in 1981 was due. I was encouraged to publish my article by Colgate-Rochester's Professor of History Emeritus Winthrop S. Hudson, as well as by the City Historian Emeritus Blake McKelvey.

Rev. Robert F. McNamara

Bibliography: Writings of (Reverend) Robert F. McNamara

Note: I think that this list covers everything of importance. I have used the following abbreviations: AER (*American Ecclesiastical Review*); CHR (*Catholic Historical Review*); CW (*Catholic World*); HPR (*Homiletic and Pastoral Review*); HRS (*Historical Records and Studies*, U.S. Catholic Historical Society); LA (*Liturgical Arts*); RACHS (*Records of the American Catholic Historical Society*); RHE (*Revue d'histoire écclésiastique*, Louvain).

Robert F. McNamara

1928

Article: "Robert McNamara Writes of Trip." *Evening Leader,* Corning, NY, July 20, 1928.

1931

Editor-in-Chief: *Georgetown College Journal* 60 (1931-32), Washington, D.C.

1932

Article: "Phases of American Religion in Thornton Wilder and Willa Cather." CW 135 (1932), pp. 641-49.

Poems: "Sonnet to T.A." (p. 10) and "Song" (p. 21) in *Measure,* Georgetown University (Washington, D.C.), Vol. 1, No. 2 (Christmas 1932).

1937

Article: "The University of the Sacred Heart, Milan." *Georgetown French Review* (Washington, D.C.), Vol. 1, No. 1 (January, 1937).

1941

Appendix: "Archdiocesan and Diocesan Sees of the Latin Rite in the United States and Their Occupants" in Theodore Maynard, *The Story of American Catholicism*. New York, 1941, pp. 617-48.

1943

Article: "Corpus Domini: Some Notes on Eucharistic Miracles." AER 108 (1943), pp. 415-28.

Booklet: "St. Bernard's Seminary 1893-1943." *The Sheaf: Golden Jubilee Edition*. Rochester, NY: St. Bernard's Alumni Association, 1943.

1944

Article: "Trusteeism in the Atlantic States, 1785-1863." CHR 30 (1944-1945), pp. 135-54.

1945

Article: "War-Mother: the Madonna of Humility Street." CW 161 (1945), pp. 230-36.

Translated article: Cardinal Pierre d'Ailly, "The Twelve Honors Which God Bestowed on St. Joseph." *St. Joseph's Lilies* (St. Joseph's Convent, Toronto, Can.) 34 (1945), pp. 22-25.

1946

Column: "The Good Old Days," *Evening Leader*, Corning, NY. Seventy articles, unsigned ("The Old Chronicler"), in three series leading to and following the Corning centennial of incorporation: Series I, December 14, 1946, to June 28, 1947; Series II, October 14, 1947 to June 19, 1948; Series III, September 18, 1948, to December 23, 1948.

1947

Book review: John Tracy Ellis, *A Select Bibliography of the History of the Catholic Church in the United States*. AER 117 (1947), p.756.

Lecture: "The Upper Chemung Valley and the American Revolution," to Corning-Painted Post (NY) Historical Society, unpublished.

1948

Book review: Theodore Maynard, *A Fire Was Lighted: The Life of Rose Hawthorne Lathrop*. CHR 34 (1948-1949), pp. 183-84.

Book review: Sr. Hildegard Yeager, C.S.C., *The Life of James Roosevelt Bayley*. AER 108 (1948), pp. 396-97.

Booklet (unsigned): *Golden Jubilee, Saint Augustine's Church, Rochester, New York*. Published by the parish, 1948.

Book: *A Century of Grace: The History of St. Mary's Roman Catholic Parish, Corning, NY, 1848-1948*. Published by the parish, 1948.

1950

Book review: Blake McKelvey, *Rochester, The Flower City, 1885-1890*. CHR 36 (1950-1951), pp. 364-65.

Article:"Blessed Bernardine of the Pious Pawnshops." *St. Joseph's Lilies* (St. Joseph's Convent, Toronto, Can.) 39 (1950), pp. 215-19.

Note (unsigned) on consecration of Archbishop Jeremiah J. Harty. CHR 35 (1949-50), pp. 480-81.

Note (unsigned) on consecration of Bishop Thomas A. Hendrick. CHR 35 (1949-50), pp. 205-06.

Note (unsigned) on consecration of Bishop Frederick Z. Rooker. CHR 36 (1950-1951), p. 237.

Article: "Father Maurice of Greece. NY: A Footnote to the Liberian Mission." RACHS 61 (1950), pp. 155-83.

1951

Book review: J. H. Kennedy, *Jesuit and Savage in New France*. CHR 36 (1950-1951), p. 470-71.

Book review: *Félix Klein, La route du petit Morvandiau. Souvenirs* VI, CHR 37 (1951-1952), pp. 44-45.

Note (unsigned) on U.S. prelates who attended the papal definitions of the Immaculate Conception and the Assumption. CHR 37 (1951-1952), pp. 55-56.

1952

Book review: James Hastings Nichols, *Democracy and the Churches*. CHR 38 (1952-1953), pp. 331-33.

Note (unsigned) on the date of ordination of Cardinal William H. O'Connell. CHR 38 (1952-1953), pp. 55-56.

Article (editor) of Cardinal Raphael Merry del Val, "Towards a Holier Priesthood." AER 129 (1953), pp. 290-94.

Article: "Good-by to Humility Street." *America* 90 (1953), pp. 39-41.

Article: "Dal Rione Trevi al Gianicolo." *Ecclesia* (Vatican City: Vatican Polyglot Press) 12 (1953), pp. 485-86.

Article: "Pope Pius IX and the Accident at St. Agnes." *Ave Maria* 78 (1953), pp. 17-19.

Book review: Joseph McSorley, C.S.P., *Father Hecker and His Friends.* CHR 39 (1953-1954), pp. 62-63.

1954

Booklet: *A Hundred Years of Service: St. Patrick's Church, Mumford, New York.* Published by the parish, 1954.

Article: "The North American College." *Jubilee*, Vol. 1, No. 12 (April 1954), pp. 35-39.

Note (unsigned) on the opening of the new North American College buildings, Vatican City. CHR 40 (1954-1955), pp. 93-94.

Note (unsigned) on the curriculum vitae of Abbot Bernard Smith, O.S.B. (1812-1892). CHR 40 (1954-1955), pp. 94-96.

Book review: Emilio Bonomelli, *I Papi in Campagna.* CHR 40 (1954-1955), pp. 299-301.

Founding moderator-editor: *The Sheaf* (alumni-student annual, St. Bernard's Seminary, Rochester, NY), 1954-1981.

1955

Preface: Joseph J. Baierl, tr. and ed., *The Catholic Church and the Modern State, A Study of Their Mutual Juridical Claims.* Rochester, NY, 1955.

Book review: Dorothy G. Wayman, *Cardinal O'Connell of Boston: A Biography of William Henry O'Connell, 1859-1944.* CHR 41 (1955-1956), pp. 190-91.

1956

Book review: Fredegandus Callaey, O.F.M. Cap. *Praelectiones Historiae Ecclesiasticae Aetatis Recentioris et Praesentis.* CHR 42 (1956-1957), pp. 173-74.

Book: *The American College in Rome, 1855-1955.* Rochester, NY: Christopher Press, Inc., 1956.

1957

Article (with William A. Trott): "Apostle of the Pen: Joseph Baierl, S.T.D." *The Sheaf* 1957 (St. Bernard's Seminary, Rochester, N.Y.), pp. 10-15.

Book review: Robert Sylvain, *La vie et l'oeuvre de Henry de Courcy (1820-1861). The Americas* 13 (1957), pp. 322-24.

Preface: John M. Daley, S.J., *Georgetown College: Origin and Early Years.* Washington, D.C.: Georgetown University Press, 1957.

1958

Leaflet on the symbolism of the nave windows of St. Louis Church, Pittsford, NY. Published by the parish, 1958.

Book review: M.L.W. Laistner, *The Intellectual Heritage of the Middle Ages. The Priest* 14 (1958), pp. 252-53.

Book review: Zsolt Aradi, *Pius XI, the Pope and the Man. The Priest* 14 (1958), pp. 951-52.

1959

Article: "Checklist for Chalices." *The Priest* 15 (1959), pp. 48-53.

Article: "Minor Basilicas in the United States." HPR 59 (1958-1959), pp. 907-12.

Book review: Vincent F. Holden, C.S.P., *The Yankee Paul: Isaac Thomas Hecker.* CHR 44 (1958-1959), pp. 471-73.

Articles: "Yesterday's Romans" (pp. 86-93) and "The Everydays" (pp. 160-71). *Roman Echoes: College Centennial 1859-1959* (Rome, Italy, North American College), 1959.

Article: "The Benjamin Patterson Bridge in Steuben County." *New York History* 40 (1959), pp. 62-64.

1960

Book Review: Thomas O. Hanley. S.J., *Their Rights and Liberties: The Beginnings of Religious and Political Freedom in Maryland. Georgetown Alumni Magazine,* January 1960.

Book review: John D. Sauter, *The American College of Louvain (1857-1898).* RHE 55 (1960), pp. 624-26.

Funeral eulogy on Rev. Frederick J. Zwierlein. *Catholic Courier Journal,* Rochester, NY, Oct. 14, 1960.

Booklet: *St. Columba's Church, Caledonia, New York, 1885-1960.* Published by the parish, 1960.

1961

Articles (13) on Rochester Diocese and the Civil War: *Catholic Courier Journal,* Rochester, NY, Jan. 6, 1961, to Apr. 8, 1965.

Book review: H. A. Reinhold, *Bringing the Mass to the People.* LA 29 (1960-61), p. 58.

Book review: Francis Borgia Steck, O.F.M., *Marquette Legends.* RHE 56 (1961), pp. 561-650.

Booklet: *History of Sacred Heart Cathedral, Rochester, New York.* Published by the parish, 1961.

Obituary notice (unsigned) of Rev. Frederick J. Zwierlein. CHR 46 (1960-1961), pp. 506-07.

Book review: Francis P. Weisenburger, *Founded on Faith: The Crisis of Church-Going America, 1865-1900.* CHR 47 (1961-1962), pp. 47-48.

Booklet: *St. Mary's Hospital and the Civil War.* Published by St. Mary's Hospital, Rochester, NY, 1961.

Ed., *Student Register, North American College Rome, 1859-1959* (revised and augmented). Rochester NY: Christopher Press, Inc., 1961.

1962

Article: "Open Letter to an Architect," LA 30 (1961-1962), pp. 120-22.

Book review: Peter Canisius van Lierde, O.E.S.A., *The Holy See at Work.* LA 30 (1961-1962), p. 144.

Article: "'Conopoeum and Tintinnabulum, the Basilican Insignia." LA 31 (1962-1963), pp. 29-31.

Book review: Joseph A. Jungmann, S.J., *Pastoral Liturgy*. LA 31 (1962-1963), p. 33.

Book review: Reginald Masterson, O.P., *Theology in the Catholic College*. LA 31 (1962-1963), pp. 59-61.

Book review: Michael J. Taylor, S.J., *The Protestant Liturgical Revival: A Catholic Viewpoint*. LA 31 (1962-1963), pp. 92-93.

Article: "Father Jean Dilhet: His Visit to Western New York." HRS 49 (1962), pp. 77-85.

1963

Book review: Henry J. Koren, C.S.Sp., *Knave of Knights? A History of the Spiritan Missions in Acadia and North America*. RHE 58 (1963), pp. 230-32.

Article: "Archbishop Hanna, Rochesterian," *Rochester History* 25, No. 2 (Rochester Public Library), 1963.

Book review: Francis L. Broderick, *Right Reverend New Dealer: John A. Ryan*. CHR 49 (1963-1964), pp. 247-48.

Article (with Robert J. Miller): "Edward J. Byrne, Biblical Scholar." *The Sheaf 1963* (St. Bernard's Seminary, Rochester, NY), pp. 19-26.

Article: "Etats-Unis d'Amérique." *Dictionnaire d'histoire et de géographie écclésiastique* (Paris), 15 (1963), cols. pp. 1109-47.

Book review: Paul Claudel, *I Believe in God: A Meditation on the Apostles' Creed*. LA 32 (1963-1964), pp. 33-34

Guest editorial: "Again... An American Ambassador to the Vatican?" *Catholic Courier Journal*, Rochester, NY, Aug. 9, 1963.

1964

Article: "Fast and Abstinence: a Fresh Start?" HPR 65 (1963-1964), pp. 219-21.

1965

Book review: Eric Peterson, *The Angels and the Liturgy*. LA 33 (1964-1965), p. 99.

Book review: John A. T. Robinson, *Liturgy Coming to Life*. LA 33 (1964-1965), p. 134.

Book review: H. Fesquet, *Catholicism: Religion of Tomorrow?* LA 33 (1964-65), p. 137.

Articles: *Catholic Encyclopedia for School and Home*, 1965: "North American College"; "Rochester, Diocese of"; "Trusteeism."

Article: "N.C.W.C.: a Forum Achieved." *Continuum*, 2 (1965), pp. 638-43.

Lecture (unpublished): "Corning, New York: 'No Mean City," delivered to Corning-Painted Post (NY) Historical Society, May 6, 1965.

1966

Book review: Bernard J. Cook, S.J., *Christian Sacraments and Christian Personality*, LA 34 (1965-1966), p.61.

Book review: Annibale Bugnini, C.M., Ed., *The Commentary on the Constitution and the Instruction on the Sacred Liturgy.* LA 34 (1965-1966), pp. 65-66.

Book review: George E. O'Donnell, *Saint Charles Seminary, Philadelphia.* CHR 52 (1966-1967), pp. 444-45.

Article: "Doctor Goggin: a Dedicated Life." *The Sheaf* (St. Bernard's Seminary, Rochester, NY), 1957, pp. 3-8, 56.

Booklet (unsigned): *Vigil Service for a Deceased Priest.* Liturgical Commission of the Diocese of Rochester, 1966.

Articles (27) on aspects of Rochester diocesan history: *Catholic Courier Journal*, Rochester, NY, October 14, 1966, to March 7, 1969.

1967

Booklet: *Annunciation Parish. The First Fifty Years.* Published by the Church of the Annunciation, Rochester, NY, 1967.

Articles: *New Catholic Encyclopedia*, 1967: "Crib"; "Edes, Ella B;" "Heortology"; "Lambert, Louis Aloysius"; "Macnutt, Francis Augustus"; "McQuaid, Bernard John"; "North American College"; "Rochester, Diocese of"; "Schulte, Augustine Joseph"; "Schuster, Ildefonso"; "Stational Church"; "Trusteeism."

Article: "How Our Divisions [denominational] Were Begun." *Catholic Courier Journal*, Rochester, NY, May 12, 1967.

1968

Book: *The Diocese of Rochester, 1868-1968.* Published by the Diocese, 1968.

Booklet: *St. Bernard's Seminary, 1893-1968*. 1968 issue of *The Sheaf*, published by St. Bernard's Seminary, Rochester, NY.

Book review: David F. Sweeney, O.F.M., *The Life of John Lancaster Spalding*. CHR 53 (1967-1968), pp. 634-36.

Article: "An Early American Missionary [Patrick O'Kelly]." *St. Kieran's College Record* 1968 (St. Kieran's College, Kilkenny), pp. 25-26.

1969

Article: "When LaSalle Visited Irondequoit Bay, 1669." *Catholic Courier Journal*, Aug. 22, 1969.

Article: "Roman, Not Latin: Our Eastern Catholic Churches." *Catholic Courier Journal*, Rochester, NY, October 17, 1969.

Article: "Monsignor Grady." *The Sheaf* (St. Bernard's Seminary, Rochester, NY), 1969, pp. 17-19.

Article: "James P. B. Duffy...an Appreciation." *Catholic Courier Journal*, Rochester, NY, July 18, 1969.

1970

Book review: Cassian J. Yuhaus, C.P., *Compelled to Speak: The Passionists in America, Origin and Apostolate*. CHR 56 (1970-1971), pp. 183-84.

Book: co-editor, Alexander M. Stewart, *French Pioneers in the Eastern Great Lakes Area, 1609-1791*. Rochester, NY, New York State Archeological Association, 1970.

1971

Book review: John P. Gallagher, *A Century of History: The Diocese of Scranton, 1868-1968*. CHR 56 (1970-1971), pp. 187-88.

Article: "Monsignor Craugh: A Memoir." *The Sheaf* 1971, pp. 3-14.

1972

Review article: "The American Priesthood: An Historical Vista." Review of John Tracy Ellis, ed., *The Catholic Priest in the United States*. AER 166 (1972), pp. 201-08.

Article: "Father Krolak, Consoler." *The Sheaf* (St. Bernard's Seminary, Rochester, NY), 1972, pp. 3-9.

1973

Article: "Theodore Maynard, Biographer of Thomas More." *Moreana* (Angers, France) 39 (1973), pp. 5-13.

Booklet: *Historic St. Mary's Church, Albany, New York.* Published by the parish, 1973.

1974

Book review: D. P. Noonan, *The Passion of Fulton Sheen.* CHR 60 (1974), p. 343.

Article: "What Would You Like to Know About the Church: Grape Juice Permitted for Mass." *Catholic Digest* 39 (1974), pp. 99-101.

Articles (24) on pilgrimage churches for Holy Year, 1974-1975: *Catholic Courier Journal*, Rochester, NY, Jan. 1, 1974, to Apr. 23, 1975.

1975

Booklet: *Catholic Bicentennial Profiles.* Rochester, NY: Christopher Press, Inc., 1975.

Article and selections in *Roman Echoes of the North American College.* Vatican City: North American College, 1975.

Monograph: *Catholic Sunday Preaching: The American Guidelines, 1791-1975.* Washington, D.C., Word of God Institute, 1975.

1976

Article: "Americans in the Service of the Vatican." In Robert Trisco, ed., *Catholics in America 1776-1976.* Washington, D.C.: National Conference of Catholic Bishops, 1976, pp. 223-28.

Article: "Who Was William Joseph Walter?" *Thomas More in America* (*Moreana*, vol. 13), Angers, France, and U.S.A., 1976, pp. 128-31.

Book, ed.: *Essays in Honor of Joseph P. Brennan.* Rochester, NY: St. Bernard's Seminary (Part I, 1976 issue of *The Sheaf,* alumni-seminary publication).

Article: "Lulworth Castle, Bicentennial Shrine." *America* 135 (1976), pp. 463-64.

1977

Article: "Programmed Homilies: No-no or Necessity?" HPR 77 (Feb. 1977), pp. 25-32.

Cassette: "Programmed Homilies: No-no or Necessity?" (same as above), Cardinal Publications.

Book review: Robert T. Handy, *A History of the Churches in the United States and Canada. The Tablet* (London, England) 231 (Apr. 2, 1977), p. 329.

Book review: Sister Mary Christine Taylor, S.S.J., *A History of the Foundations of Catholicism in Northern New York.* CHR 63 (1977), pp. 629-31.

1978

Article: "How Not to Preach: Some Lurid Examples." HPR 78 (May 1978), pp. 27-32.

Article: "Elmira Heights Catholic Parishes." In Thomas E. Byrne, ed., *Chemung County, 1890-1975.* Elmira, NY: Chemung County Historical Society, 1978, pp. 419-31.

1979

Booklet: *Mother of Sorrows, Rochester, New York.* Published by the parish, 1979.

Homilies: HPR 79 (1978-1979), No. 6, pp. 33-45.

Homilies: HPR 80 (1979-1980), No. 3, pp. 33-46.

Article: "What Is a Homily?" HPR 79 (1978-1979), Aug.-Sept. 1979, pp. 40-47.

Article, ed.: "McQuaid's Sermon on Theological Americanism." RACHS 90 (1979), pp. 23-32.

Article: "St. Elizabeth Ann Seton. Her Shrine at St. Thomas the Apostle Church [Rochester]." Published by the parish, 1979.

Book: *A Century of Grace: The History of St. Mary's Roman Catholic Parish, Corning, NY, 1848-1948.* Second edition, slightly revised. Published by the parish, 1979.

Book reviews: Martin J. Becker, *A History of Catholic Life in the Diocese of Albany, 1669-1864;* and Sr. Mary Christine Taylor, S.S.J., *A History of the Foundations of Catholicism in Northern New York.* RHE 74, No.1 (1979), pp. 123-25.

1980

Letter to editor: "Liturgy as Politics." *America* 142 (1980), p. 29.

Article: "Charles Carroll of Belle Vue, Co-founder of Rochester." *Rochester History* 42, No. 4, October 1980.

1981

Book review: Michael E. Williams, *The Venerable English College, Rome.* CHR 67 (1981), pp. 148-49.

Article: "Charles Carroll: State Street Once Bore His Name." *Upstate (Democrat and Chronicle,* Rochester, NY), December 6, 1981, pp. 51-53.

1982

Booklet: *Saint Thomas the Apostle Church: The First Sixty Years, 1922-1982.* Published by the parish, 1982.

1983

Book review: Andrea Riccardi, "Roma! Citta Sacra? Dalla Conciliazione all' operazione Sturzo" (Milano Vita e Pensiero, 1979). CHR, LXIX (1983), pp. 64-66.

Booklet: *Along the Royal Road: Christ the King Parish, Rochester, New York, 1957-1982.* Published by the parish, 1983.

Book reviews: Michael O'Carroll, C.S.Sp., *Pius XII: Greatness Dishonoured. A Documented Study;* Bernard R. Bonnot, *Pope John XXIII: An Astute Pastoral Leader;* Paul Johnson, *Pope John Paul II and the Catholic Restoration.* CHR LXIX (1983), pp. 448-49.

Articles on the Holy Year of Redemption (28) in *Catholic Courier Journal,* July 27, 1983, to April 18, 1984. Historical accounts of pilgrimage churches in diocese, plus others historical ("Holy Years of Yore in the Diocese," Jan. 11, 1984) and devotional (e.g., "Indulgences," Feb. 15, 1984).

1984

Leaflet: "Holy Sepulchre Cemetery, Rochester, New York." Published 1984 by the cemetery, in connection with the Rochester City Sesquicentennial.

Book review: Florence D. Cohalan, *A Popular History of the Archdiocese of New York. New York History* 55 (1984), pp. 111-12.

Booklet: *William Frisby Fitzhugh, Co-founder of Rochester.* Published by the Rochester Historical Society, Genesee Country Occasional Papers, Vol. XVI, Rochester, NY, 1984.

Book review: Thomas H. O'Connor, *Fitzpatrick's Boston, 1846-1866. America* 151 (1984), pp. 407-08.

1985

Article: "In Search of the Carrolls of Belle Vue." *Maryland Historical Magazine* 80 (1985), pp. 99-113.

Book review: Mel Phiel, *Breaking Bread: The Catholic Worker and the Origin of Catholic Radicalism in America. Agape* (Rochester Catholic Worker at Bethany House) 1, No. 3, Spring 1985, pp. 6, 8.

Article: "John Carroll and Interfaith Marriages: The Case of the Belle Vue Carrolls." In Nelson H. Minnich, Robert B. Eno, S.S., and Robert F. Trisco, *Studies in Catholic History in Honor of John Tracy Ellis.* Wilmington, Delaware: Michael Glazier, 1985, pp. 27-59.

Book review: Richard Shaw, *John Dubois, Founding Father.* RHE 80, No. 3-4 (1985), pp. 917-19.

1986

Book review: Joseph P. Chinnici, O.F.M., Ed., *Devotion to the Holy Spirit in American Catholicism.* CHR LXII, 1986, pp. 514-15.

Article: "Colonel Fitzhugh's Pickle." *Genesee Country Companion* (Newsletter, Genesee Country Museum; Mumford, NY) Vol. 6, No. 8 (October 1986), p.3

Booklet: *History of Sacred Heart Cathedral Parish, Rochester, New York, 1911-1986*, Frederick L. Bonisteel, co-author. Updated and republished for the Diamond Jubilee Committee by the Cathedral Parish, 1986. (A revision of *History of Sacred Heart Cathedral*, Rochester, New York, published for the golden jubilee. See above under 1961.)

Article: "A Jubilarian Reflects on the Declining Number of Priests."
America 155 (1986), pp. 381- 383, 385.

1987

Book review: Robert E. Sullivan and James M. O'Toole, eds., *Catholic Boston: Studies in Religion and Community, 1870-1970*. RHE, Vol. 82, No. 2 (April – June 1987), pp. 326-29.

Book review: David O'Brien, *Faith and Friendship: Catholicism in the Diocese of Syracuse, 1886-1896*. Sidebar stories by Ronald D. Smith (Syracuse: The Catholic Diocese of Syracuse, 1987). *New York History* LXVIII, No. 4 (October 1987), pp. 434-35.

1988

Book review: David O'Brien, *Faith and Friendship: Catholicism in the Diocese of Syracuse, 1886-1896*. Sidebar stories by Ronald D. Smith (Syracuse: The Catholic Diocese of Syracuse, 1987). CHR LXXIV, No. 1 (January 1988), pp.133-34.

1989

Article: "Religious Vocations: A Family Concern." *The Priest* 45, No. 8 (August 1989), pp.7-8.

Book review: Marvin R. O'Connell, *John Ireland and the American Catholic Church. Canadian Catholic Review* 7 (July/August 1989), p. 265.

1990

Articles: *Dictionary of Christianity in America*, Intervarsity Press, Downers Grove, IL, January 1990: "McQuaid, Bernard John (1823-1909)"; "North American College"; "The Pontifical."

Book review: John Tracy Ellis. *Faith and Learning, A Church Historian's Story*. CHR LXXVI (1990), pp. 93-94.

Article: "A Reflection: A Cross, Easily Seen." *America* 162 (1990), P. 307.

Booklet: *Jack Mack; or The Shooting of Ellen Callinan, A Forgotten Corning Tragedy*. An Occasional Paper for the Centennial of the City of Corning. Corning, NY: Corning-Painted Post Historical Society, 1990.

Article: "Ecumenism and the Rochester Center for Theological Studies." *Rochester History* LII (Fall 1990), No. 4, pp. 21-22.

Article: "A Nun's View of Rochester, 1848." *Rochester History*, LII (Fall 1990), No. 4, pp. 22-28.

Book review: Susan J. White, *Art, Architecture and Liturgical Reform*. CHR LXXVI (1990), pp. 896-98.

1991

Article: "Old-Style Family Physician: Corning's 'Doc Mac' (1856-1927)." *The Crooked Lake Review* (Hammondsport, NY), No. 34 (January 1991), pp. 14-15, 22; No. 35 (February 1991), pp.14-15, 21; No. 36 (March 1991), pp. 14-16; No. 37 (April 1991), pp. 15-16.

Skit (with co-authors Rev. Daniel P. Tormey and Rev. Albert L. Delmonte): "The Return of Bishop McQuaid," presented before the Rochester Diocesan Convocation of Priests at the Corning Hilton, April 8, 1991. Unpublished.

Book review: Joseph Durkin, S.J., ed., *Swift Potomac's Lovely Daughter: Two Centuries at Georgetown through Students' Eyes*. CHR LXXVII (1991), pp.547-48.

Article: "Rockwell's Civil War 'Henry': The Rifle and the Rifleman." *The Crooked Lake Review* (Hammondsport, NY), No. 44 (November 1991), pp. 1, 11-12; No. 45 (December 1991), pp. 5-6, 16-17; No. 46 (January 1992), pp. 5-6, 18; No. 47 (February 1992), pp. 12-13.

1992

Article: "Rochester Boasts Unassuming Civil War Hero." *Catholic Courier* (Rochester, NY), July 2, 1992, p. 5.

Book review: Josyp Terelya with Michael H. Brown, *Witness to Apparitions and Persecutions in the USSR*. *Catholic Courier* (Rochester, NY), October 9, 1992, p. 13.

Article: "Corning's Memorable Maestro: Charles C. Corwin (1883-1954)." *The Crooked Lake Review* (Hammondsport, NY), No. 55 (October 1992), pp. 1, 8, 9, 10; No. 56 (November 1992), pp. 8, 9, 10; No. 57 (December 1992), pp. 11, 12; No. 58 (January 1993), pp. 11-13; No. 59 (February 1993), pp. 11-13.

Book review: Daniel Donovan, *What Are They Saying about the Ministerial Priesthood? Catholic Courier* (Rochester, NY), December 10, 1992, p. 8.

1993

Book review: Thomas Day, *Why Catholics Can't Sing: The Culture of Catholicism and the Triumph of Bad Taste. Catholic Courier* (Rochester, NY), Feb. 11, 1993, p. 9.

Book review: Michael H. Brown, *The Final Hour: The Century of Good Versus Evil. Catholic Courier* (Rochester, NY), April 15, 1993, p. 16.

Article: "How We Rediscovered Canada in 1928." *The Crooked Lake Review* (Hammondsport, NY), No. 67 (October 1993), pp. 1, 17-19; No. 68 (November 1993), pp. 11-13; No. 69 (December 1993), pp. 11-12; No. 70 (January 1994), pp.11-13. (See above, 1928.)

1994

Book: *Ambassadors for Christ: A Necrology of Priests and Permanent Deacons Who Have Served within the Diocese of Rochester-in-America, 1818-1993.* Published by the Diocese, 1994.

Article: "Hell is Harrowed, Alleluia!" *America* 170 (May 7, 1994), pp. 16-17.

Article: "So You're Retiring, Father Jones?" *The Priest*, June 1994, pp.39-40.

Article: "Formidable Miss Fannie." *The Crooked Lake Review* (Hammondsport, NY), No. 77 (August 1994), pp. 1, 14-15.

Article: "The Ordination Controversy: A Cautionary Parallel." HPR XCV, No. 3 (December 1994), pp. 54-61.

1995

Article: "Toasting Irishwomen!" *Catholic Courier* (Rochester, NY), March 16, 1995, pp. 1, 14.

Article: "The Pitchmen; or, How a Fourteen-year-old Corningite Spent His Saturday Evenings in 1925." *The Crooked Lake Review* (Hammondsport, NY), No. 88 (July 1995), pp. 1, 12-16.

Article: "Thank you, Miss Relihan!" *The Crooked Lake Review*, (Hammondsport, NY), No. 93 (December 1995), pp. 1, 12-16.

1996

Article: "Woodcarver's Visions Grace Diocesan Churches." *Catholic Courier* (Rochester, NY), July 4, 1996, p. 5. (Wooden statues and ornamentation in Blessed Sacrament Church, Rochester, and St. Stephen's Church, Geneva, NY, by Ioannes Kirchmayer, Oberammergau-born immigrant sculptor, ca. 1860-1939).

1997

Letter to editor: "Two sides of Schuster" (Bl. Ildefonso Schuster, O.S.B., Archbishop of Milan). *The Tablet* (London UK), Feb. 15, 1997, p. 219.

Article: "Of Heaven and Earth; Priest's Art Pays Fealty to St. Mary." *Catholic Courier* (Rochester, NY), May 8, 1997, pp. 1, 16. (Altarpiece in St. Mary's Church, Dansville, by former pastor, Fr. Aloysius Somoggi, 1851-1855)

Articles: "Louis Aloysius Lambert (1835-1910)"; "Bernard John Joseph McQuaid (1823-1909);" In Michael Glazier and Thomas J. Shelley, eds, *The Encyclopedia of American Catholic History*, Collegeville, MN (1997), pp. 792-93, 895-96.

1998

Book: The *Diocese of Rochester in America, 1868-1993*. Second edition of *The Diocese of Rochester, 1868-1968*, emended and updated to include 125 years of the Diocese's existence. Published by the Diocese, 1998.

Book: *Good Old Doctor Mac: Thomas A. McNamara, Family Physician 1856-1927*. Utica, NY: Devon Press, 2004.

Breastplate of St. Patrick

I arise today
Through the strength of Christ's birth with His baptism,
Through the strength of His crucifixion with His burial,
Through the strength of His resurrection with His ascension,
Through the strength of His descent for the judgment of doom.

Christ with me,
Christ before me,
Christ behind me,
Christ in me,
Christ beneath me,
Christ above me,
Christ on my right,
Christ on my left,
Christ when I lie down,
Christ when I sit down,
Christ when I arise,
Christ in the heart of every man who thinks of me,
Christ in the mouth of everyone who speaks of me,
Christ in every eye that sees me,
Christ in every ear that hears me.

Interviews for *A Priest Forever*

Jeanne Marie Bello
July 4, 2003

Bishop Matthew Clark
August 5, 2003

Rev. Francis Davis
April 25, 2003

Sandra Doran
April 12, 2003, and February 17, 2006

Noel Drower (niece of Father McNamara)
February 6, 2006

Rev. Sebastian Falcone
June 2005

Rev. William Graf
February 16, 2004

Rev. Joseph Hart
August 27, 2003

Rev. Thomas Hoctor
June 24, 2003

Dr. Joseph Kelly
February 2003

Msgr. Gerard Krieg
June 13, 2003

Rev. Robert C. MacNamara
June 2, 2003

Rev. Robert F. McNamara
September 26, 2003; August 5, 2005; February 23, 2006

Msgr. J. Emmett Murphy
July 1, 2003

Mary Napoleon
May 2003

Rev. Celestine Obi
August 5, 2005

Twilla O'Dell (Steuben County
Historian)
June 14, 2004

Rev. Jasper Pennington
May 15, 2004

Rev. John Philipps
June 27, 2003

Rev. John Reif
November 2005

Sister Roberta Rodenhouse,
R.S.M.
January 27, 2004

Victoria Schmitt
July 14, 2003

Msgr. William Shannon
June 26, 2003

Sister Anna Louise Staub, S.S.J
June 26, 2003

Rev. Conrad Sundholm
June 13, 2003

Ida and Samuel Turan
February 29, 2004

Kathleen Urbanic
June 26, 2003

Archival Collections Consulted

Archives of the Diocese of Rochester, NY
Georgetown University Archives
Archives of the Pontifical North American College

About the Author

Ann K. Maloney earned a master's degree in social work from the National Catholic School of Social Service at Catholic University of America. Retired after working for more than thirty years in children and family services in New York, she is actively writing children's stories focusing on peace and justice.

Made in the USA
Middletown, DE
29 July 2016